To: Sandra

with every good wish

W Clark Ellzey

December 1964

*Preparing
Your
Children
for
Marriage*

A MANUAL FOR PARENTS

by

W. Clark Ellzey

Preparing
Your
Children
for
Marriage

ASSOCIATION PRESS NEW YORK

Publisher's stock number: 1555

Library of Congress catalog card number: 64-19745

 72

Printed in the United States of America

To Elly Maria,
who struggled with me through
the privileges and responsibilities of parenthood;
to Jane, Sandy, and Bill,
beneficiaries and victims of our efforts;
to Tom,
who came to us already grown,
and had to accept us as graduate parents.

Author's Preface

THE CIRCUMSTANCES in which a couple establish a home today are radically different from those of just a few years ago. Increased mobility brings young people together in marriage from very different backgrounds more frequently than in the past. They enter marriage with quite different ideas of what marriage is, of what a husband is and how he deals with his wife, of what a wife is and how she deals with her husband, of what parenthood is and how parents deal with their children.

There is some question whether the home of today prepares the young for marriage as well as the home of yesterday. Prior to the turn of the century family life was more alike all over the nation than it is today. The pseudopatriarchal family form was almost universal. Images of husband, wife, father, mother, and child were more standardized and much clearer. The young had easily recognizable models to observe and imitate. Growing up in such a home was considered sufficient preparation for marriage.

With the disruptive effects of the technological explosion and its consequent cultural revolution, it has become apparent that a more formal study-approach to marriage may be necessary. A considerable body of knowledge has emerged from research undertaken over the past fifty years. A part of this research shows how parents, in dealing with their children from infancy until the time they leave home, are preparing them for marriage, good, bad, and indifferent.

This book is an attempt to point out some specific ways in which we as parents prepare our children for marriage, as we deal with them through the childhood years, and continue to make a contribution as our children emerge from childhood into youth. It is an attempt to point out certain ways in which children grow and develop significantly for marriage and how parents may influence the process. The author sees in this influence and in this process preparation for marriage in the home.

The reader will recognize that many forces are at work in addition to parental influence in the lives of children. Relations with brothers and sisters are involved. Other children outside the home play a part. Teachers and other adults with whom a child comes in contact also make their contribution. Housing and all else in the environment contribute in many ways. Still, according to those who study ways in which adult behavior is influenced by childhood experiences, parents play a very important and in some ways a determining part.

The materials in this book are based upon some thirty years of teaching and counseling experience in the field of marriage and family life. During that time the author has read a considerable number of research reports. He is indebted to former students who communicated their thoughts and feelings to him as they responded to their recollections of their childhood experiences in their homes and as their behavior reflected those experiences. The author's students have made contributions through personal interviews and responses to surveys after they were married and began to have families of their own. Clients who came for marriage counseling have revealed repeatedly the influence of childhood experiences on their adult behavior. The ways in which they reacted to their parents as children were recognized as influencing the ways in which they reacted to their husbands and wives in their marriages.

Membership of the author in professional organizations, such as the National Council on Family Relations, conversations and correspondence with colleagues in colleges and universities, and insights shared in the American Association of Marriage Counselors have contributed to the preparation of this book.

It is hoped that those parents who read it may be made more conscious of some specific ways in which they are preparing their children for marriage as they deal with them through the childhood period and the years of youth.

Contents

Contents

*Preparing
Your
Children
for
Marriage*

1

*What
Is
Preparation
for
Marriage?*

A FEW YEARS AGO a mother was on a train en route for a visit with her son and his family. She fell into conversation with a woman across the aisle. As frequently happens, the talk finally shifted around to families. When the mother mentioned that she had a son on the faculty of a college, the other woman inquired about his field. When the mother replied that he taught "education for marriage," the woman looked startled and after a moment inquired: "What on earth does he tell them after the first class meeting?"

Traditional Attitudes

Her attitude is understandable since formal education for marriage is a relatively recent development. For many it is an entirely new idea. Most of us had no exposure to any such educational opportunity. Our parents certainly were not exposed. For centuries just growing up in the home was considered adequate preparation for marriage. If a boy learned to work and showed any competency at it and if a girl learned to keep house and cook, this was looked upon as sufficient preparation for marriage. With strong moral and religious supports for staying married, divorce almost impossible, and the new generation's experience with marriage and family little more than a duplication of the previous generation's experience, such preparation was considered adequate.

When the idea of education or preparation for marriage was considered at all, it was conceived of as a few last words of advice. "Take good care of her." "Don't both of you get angry at the same time." "If she becomes emotional be firm with her." "If he looks at other women make him jealous." Any idea of understanding the meaning of behavior was at the level of symptoms or signs, never in terms of depth psychology. Well-meaning parents, vicariously experiencing some of the moonlight and roses of their son's or daughter's approaching wedding might nevertheless feel constrained to shake their heads sadly and say, "It's not all moonlight and roses."

More earnestly, but also more dangerously, some mother might pick out what she dislikes in her marriage and about her husband and admonish her daughter to be careful not to get herself into the same fix. Some father, responding to his wife and marriage similarly, might make comments which add up to the conclusion that all women are impossible and though you can't live with them, you can't live without them. In any case, for many people the idea of preparing their children for marriage does not emerge until a wedding is imminent. They do not seem to know that they have already done almost all that they are going to be able to do to prepare their children for marriage since they have lived with them and influenced them from birth to this wedding day. Perhaps ninety per cent of the preparation of their children will have been through demonstration in their own marriage. By comparison we teach very little "by word of mouth." There is considerable appropriateness to the old saying, "What you are speaks so loud I can't hear what you say."

This does not mean that discussion of marriage is useless within the family. The risk is that logic may be destroyed by the process of arguing from the specific to the general. Our own marriage is the basis of our own authority and it is a noticeable fact that "everybody considers himself an authority on marriage." Actually everybody is not even an authority on his own marriage since most people do not understand themselves or why they do what they do, the basic causes or the underlying motives in their marriage relationships.

A More Modern View

Many textbooks have been written for high school and college students dealing with preparation for marriage in our modern world. An increasing number of books are being published which are intended for parents. We can take advantage of these texts, some of which are listed under "For Suggested Reading" at the end of this book. Many parents have made use of them and have expressed appreciation for such assistance. These resources are valuable because they are based upon research into hundreds and thousands of marriages. But there is another way by which we might approach the problem of preparing our children for marriage. We might examine how we are presently doing it.

What is preparation for any enterprise? Suppose, instead of for marriage, we were to think of preparation for law or medicine or the field of business or farming, or the professions of teaching and the ministry. It would not make much difference. The principles concerning preparation to function in the enterprise are much the same.

If we were to look into it, we would probably find that somebody had made quite a study of the matter and drawn up a list of qualifications. This list would be based on observation of those who were successful in it and what made them successful, and of those who were not so successful, or failed, and what contributed to their failure. With such a list anyone could then estimate approximate readiness for the enterprise. As parents we might use the list of qualifications as a guide in dealing with our children. We would want to help them develop those abilities required to meet the qualifications for whatever vocation or profession for which they wanted to prepare.

Years of teaching and counseling lead the observer to conclude that there are qualifications which any person proposing to marry should have if he expects to be very successful and happy in it. This presentation is admittedly an oversimplification. You may think of other qualifications as you read along through these pages, but certain elements are clear.

No marriage is any better or any worse than the people in it. No marriage ever succeeds or fails. Success and failure are processes as well as finalities. Each may be a matter of degree. The point here is that it is the people in the marriage who succeed or fail. The degree to which they succeed or fail depends to a great measure upon their personality resources. If they have the appropriate maturity to meet and deal with the requirements for any reasonably successful marriage in today's world, they will achieve well enough and be happy most of the time. If they do not have the resources, they will not achieve and they cannot be happy. We may consider such resources qualifications in attempting to answer the question, "What is preparation for marriage?"

We could make a list such as this: "He must be kind and considerate. He must be able to hold a job. She must be able to manage her housework and not run home to mother when she gets upset." Whatever the list, what we would be talking about would be signs of maturity or immaturity. In this book therefore, we are attempting to get to the bottom of the problem. We shall be digging around among the roots of preparation and education for marriage, not climbing out on limbs and looking at the leaves.

Becoming Responsibly Independent

In observing those people who seem to be most successful and happy in their marriages, one can recognize an unusual amount of responsible independence. They need each other and they depend upon each other, but not in the way that children need parents. Their need and dependence is complementary and contributes to the enrichment and the fulfillment of their life. They have grown up.

In becoming responsibly independent, they learned all the way through childhood and youth how to take care of themselves physically. They learned what kind of food and how much their body needed. They learned how much rest was required to keep them at top efficiency. They learned the importance of exercise and were careful to make sure that they made use of such activity for the highest tone of alertness and vitality. Through all the growing-up years they learned about hygiene and how to keep themselves clean. They made appropriate use of doctors and hospitals, neither seeking them unnecessarily nor avoiding them foolishly.

If you could look through a marriage counselor's records you might be surprised to find how often such simple, common, everyday matters are among the roots of happiness or trouble in marriage. Here is a woman who does not know enough about the nutritional needs of her body, much less those of her husband and children. Emotional irritability and physical defects have been the result. Her lack of knowledge has certainly affected her marriage and parenthood as well.

Here is a man who knows he needs rest but rationalizes his continuing strain until he is down and out with physical or nervous breakdown. He has considered himself manly by denying that he could cave in and, in order to be a hero, has brushed off his wife's pleading that he consult a doctor. Since he was not responsibly independent enough to take his body to a doctor, his body took him to the doctor and kept him in the hospital a long time.

His immaturity caused anxiety to his wife. It sparked arguments, stirred up anger and resentment. She was understandably afraid since their economic welfare depended upon his healthy functioning in his job. Thus his immaturity created a marriage and family crisis and ran up expenses beyond resources.

People who have become responsibly independent carry their share of the load around their home. They pick up after themselves; they are alert to the work that needs doing and they participate in their share of it. This may include the house or the yard or the automobile or whatever is involved. They do not have to have jobs pointed out to them. They do not need to be told to do them. They can see for themselves what needs doing and they do it.

Such people are inclined to make their own decisions. They are not easily swayed by the feelings of others, although they do not disregard them. They are not stubborn; they simply think things through for themselves. The responsibly independent person rises to meet a crisis and seems to deal with the frustrations which arise from it without panic or bottling things up. He does not run away.

The responsibly independent people we know seem to have worked out fairly well the relationship between the individual and the family. They do not assert themselves regardless of others, nor do they permit others to dominate them. Somehow they have discovered that the survival and welfare of the individual *and* the family depend upon respecting the rights of each. Not all people develop these abilities to the same degree. They vary in the amount and demonstration of them. As the child or young person grows and develops across the years toward such responsible independence such growth *is* preparation for marriage.

Acquiring Respect for Authority

Again, looking into those marriages where people seem to be most successful, we can discover a rather strong respect for authority. This respect seems to be founded upon an understanding of the purpose and value of authority in creating and maintaining order and security in the home as well as in the community. Their attitude toward authority seems to be a deliberate choice to relate rather than submission or rebellion. As children and young people move from dependence upon their parents, teachers, and the police, to dependence upon themselves, they must transfer the authority from outside themselves to inside themselves; but in any case, they must have respect for it.

In the seemingly happy marriages, there is some realization of the relationship between responsibility and authority. In the division of labor where the husband is responsible for managing the financial affairs he has the authority to do it. If his wife handles the money, she has the authority to do it. Where the wife is responsible for the care of the children, she has authority over them. When these responsibilities are divided, corresponding authority goes with them. In such marriages there is a minimum of quarreling and bickering. Much frustration in marriage comes from having responsibility but no corresponding authority. As we help our children and young people to grow up and learn to respect authority, we *are* preparing them for marriage.

Securing Sufficient Status Feeling

We are impressed with the self-confidence and self-respect that characterize people in the more satisfying marriages with which we are acquainted. They not only seem to like each other; they like themselves. They do not think they are perfect. They are aware of ways in which they wish they were different. They recognize most of their weaknesses. They are not completely satisfied. But they have, in the main, accepted themselves and have an adequate regard for themselves. They do not feel inferior or superior except in circumstances where they actually are.

Those who have acquired sufficient status-feeling seem to be able to accept others as they are and to like them for what they are. Apparently they work well with others, finding it easy to co-operate. They do not always have to be the chairman of the committee or to have their name in the paper. It seems to be satisfying enough to them to contribute to the success of the enterprise. For a lack of such feeling there is much competition in unhappy marriages.

Some people are ambitious but not compulsively so. Their ambition seems to be tempered with a degree of contentment. There are few heart patients among them and seldom any with ulcers. They will probably live longer. They seem to take it for granted that others like them. It shows in husband-wife relationships. They are not always trying to impress each other. Where children and young people are growing up, helped by parents to develop a fair estimate of themselves and an adequate regard for themselves, they *are* being prepared for marriage.

Discovering the Joys of Giving

People in the happiest marriages seem to be able to respond to each other's needs because it is easy for them to give. Their own needs have apparently been fairly well met. At least they are not clamoring for their own fulfillment all the time. When they sense a need in each other they are willing and able to respond to it.

Children are delighted to give now and then because of the approval they get from doing it. But most of the childhood years are involved with getting. Young people may experience some of the pure joy of giving occasionally if their needs have been fairly well satisfied across the childhood years, and they do not still have to receive with a kind of desperation. They may still experience the joy of approval in the process of giving, but the emerging approval within themselves may be sufficiently self-satisfying to cause them to give not primarily for the sake of approval but for the joy of contributing to the welfare or happiness of someone else.

Look around you and see those who must still have attention or who strive desperately for recognition or who feel unappreciated, unwanted, unloved, or who must have a great deal of sympathy and constant reassurance, or who are desperate for affection. We all experience these needs; but if they have been fulfilled adequately for us in childhood, we may be able to supply them for others according to the greater need around us as we grow up. Marriage is a relationship in which giving is more conducive to happiness than getting. If young people arrive at marriage able to give, they *are* prepared for marriage in this very important respect.

Developing a Capacity to Love

There is a great variety of ideas about love and many expressions of it. Observation of marriages in which people seem to be generally happy reveals a considerable capacity to express affection. Coupled with it is an unquestionably strong caring concern. Now and then it is unconditional.

All across the years of childhood and most of the way through youth, the love problem is "income." Life is still very much self-centered, and so is love. The need to be loved and to love seems to be related to the strength of personality resources. The weaker the person the greater the need to receive demonstrations and expressions of love.

When people grow up and reach adulthood their love seems to be mostly "outgo." It is centered upon the well-being and the happiness of others. It is a great deal less possessive and much more forgiving. Somehow such people seem to have learned the difference between love and desire. As love contributes to the enrichment and fulfillment of life it must control desire. Uncontrolled desires may exploit and destroy.

If children and young people are loved adequately across the growing-up years and arrive at the time for marriage with some capacity for outgoing love they *have* experienced preparation for loving in marriage.

Untangling the Mystery of Sex

The sex taboos have been broken, and our society is saturated with sexual stimulation. Much enlightenment has resulted, but along with it has come an increasing amount of confusion and misery. There would still seem to be something of a mystery involved. It is true that we have acquired knowledge about sex from the moment of conception all the way to the grave, but apparently adequate knowledge is not so widely disseminated as it should be. We have discovered more of the part that emotions play but we are still tangled in psychological and emotional rationalizations and guilt.

In those homes where people have the healthiest sex life apparently fairly good communication exists between parents and children. Gaps of ignorance and bogs of misinformation are few and far between. More importantly, emotional attitudes within the family seem to have contributed to the least amount of guilt. Such people seem to have discovered each other with sufficient understanding. They possess a kind of love that enables them to respond to each other's sexual needs. They have worked out a basically satisfying sexual adjustment. This adjustment seems to be in a constant process of change as they continue to adventure through "the ages and stages" of life.

Where children and young people have been guided by parents with knowledge in a healthy emotional atmosphere and helped to understand the relation of responsibility to freedom in their sexual experiences parents *have been* preparing them for marriage.

Cultivating a Competent Conscience

Both religion and morality contribute to the development of conscience. In those marriages where people seem to be the happiest there is seldom a rigid attachment to crystallized dogma and doctrine. There is conviction and loyalty, but not the sort of brittleness that makes it easy to be shattered. In some unhappy marriages both religion and morality function as a jail and conscience as the jailer. Where people seem to be fairly well satisfied and happy in their relationships with each other and with their ideas of God and the universe, both religion and morality seem to be adventure trails into God's universe. Conscience is the guide.

Both authority and discipline are related to the development of conscience. Too much and too harsh discipline can result in a pathological conscience. Too little and too inconsistent authority and discipline produce an undecided and guilt-ridden adult. Many attitudes and actions in marriage are motivated by guilt. Where children and young people have been encouraged to continue in the development of their conscience the parents *have been* preparing them for marriage.

Mastering the Management of Money

There can be no question about the importance of money in our modern world. It is a kind of power and it carries status with it. Everyone wants it and everyone has to discover how to get it and how to use it. In observing marriages in general we find a considerable amount of conflict over both its acquisition and its use. In many marriages there is a battle at the end of every month because of the bills. Research shows practically no correlation between the amount of money people have and their happiness in marriage. What then is the key?

A study of those marriages where people seem to be getting along best reveals that they have learned the art of management. Upon closer observation we find that it is not only the money which they manage, but themselves. Someone has said that money talks. It talks mostly about the person concerned with it. It is interesting to note what it says.

In many instances it says that the person using it is desperately in need of attention or has an urgent need for approval. Sometimes it says that the person is weak and must try to show how powerful he is. Sometimes it says that a woman does not think she is very beautiful. Through the use of glamorous clothes and extravagant makeup she tries to prove that she is. Many times money simply says, "I am a terrible manager."

When children are introduced to money through allowances or some other plan and helped to discover its value and power, and young people are helped through jobs to understand how to secure money and what to do with it—when their growth and development results in a strong ego, they *are* experiencing preparation for marriage.

Learning to Work and Play

In our culture today some people work only for money and will attempt to get away with anything as far as the job is concerned. They do not seem to be among those who are having the best experiences in their marriages. There are others who are concerned about pay for their work but are also concerned about "a job well done." They are all too few, but there are some who will not leave the job until it is done well. Theirs is a pride in workmanship and a pride of accomplishment. The job itself acts as challenge. They seem to derive a great deal of satisfaction from the achievement involved. They do not ignore money, nor underestimate its value and importance, but it is not the most important thing in the world to them.

Where people are having a good time in their marriages a certain ability to deal with routine and monotony is present. Neither overwhelms. They have a suspicion that a good deal of the suffering associated with both is due to a state of mind. They have cultivated the kind of attitudes which reduce the threat to a minimum. Work, though meaningful and satisfying in and of itself, is also a means to a greater end, the living they do at home and elsewhere. Among the unhappy ones, even if the world does misunderstand them as being successful, work has become the end and life is subordinated to it. In some instances this goes on to a degree which amounts to slavery.

Again, among the happier ones, there is a capacity to play. Through play they achieve relaxation in a world where the pace of living has reached such speed as to create tensions which are unhealthy when they are not fatal. Whatever they do for play has the effect of recharging the batteries. It is in fact, re-creation.

In the best marriages there seems to be a fair balance between work and play. The timing is good, and the proportion is appropriate. When children and young people are helped to understand the requirements for successful work and for enjoyable play, and the art of counterbalancing the two, they *are* experiencing preparation for marriage.

Distinguishing Between Fantasy and Reality

The childhood world is full of fantasy. Children live a great deal of their life in imagination. The adult world is crammed with reality not all of which is pleasurable and conducive to happiness. The problem of growing up is partly one of moving out of the world of fantasy into the world of reality. Children do this as they develop resources for dealing with life across childhood years. The more competent they become, the more readily they face reality.

When we are afraid or fail we have a tendency to regress, to escape, or to compensate. We drift into the world of fantasy which belonged to us during childhood. We all need to escape and to compensate now and then, but when this becomes a substitute for dealing with reality we cannot expect successful and happy living in marriage or anywhere else. When children and young people can be helped out of the world of fantasy and through the world of romantic illusions in their increasing competence to deal with life as it is in the adult world, they *are* being helped to prepare for marriage.

Achieving Success and Happiness

Any observation of the most successful and the most happily married people will reveal a rather competent development of personal resources with which to deal with life in general. These resources may include others but certainly include all those previously mentioned as signs of maturity. This competence to function on an adult level with sufficient maturity is derived through the relationships and the experiences of children and young people in their homes and their communities across the years. Such growth and development equips them to deal with life, especially married life.

If one thing has emerged more clearly than any other through the author's thirty years of teaching and counseling, it is the fact that immaturity is the chief cause of trouble in marriage. Immaturity in those of us who are parents cripples and distorts our parenthood. It threatens or determines the meagerness of our own marriages. Nothing is so important in the preparation of children and young people for their coming marriages as the normal progress of their maturation process.

An appalling number of otherwise intelligent people—some of them scholars—fail to see the significance to marriage of those personality resources which make us competent as adults to deal with life in general, and which can be identified as ways in which we mature. Whatever is important to our dealing with life in general is much more important in marriage. Here is a relationship more intense and more constant than any other we ever have. It puts more strain on our personality resources than any other kind of relationship. We may be able to control our temper well enough to get along with business associates and friends, but many of us do not have enough control to enable us to get along with our husband or wife. We may be able to put on a front, to pretend or actually to deal with the outside world fairly well, but our spouse and children see through us.

This is one reason why people are so surprised when certain friends of theirs announce their intent to secure a divorce. They were doing all right with the outside world. They were mature enough for that, but not mature enough for marriage. They could fool people outside their home, but could not fool each other. Marriage neither makes us nor breaks us; it merely shows us up. And what it shows up, more significantly than anything else, is our maturity and immaturity.

As growth occurs, knowledge is acquired and skills are developed. Research in such related fields as sociology, psychology, economics, history, philosophy, religion, law, and medicine has produced much information about marriage and parenthood in our modern world. Direct study of thousands of marriages has added to the body of knowledge we now have available. As young people secure some of this knowledge of marriage in our modern society and acquire skills required for living together in such a relationship they *are* preparing for marriage.

* * * * *

As parents we help our children and we hinder them as they struggle to become responsibly independent, to acquire respect for authority, to secure status feeling, to discover the joys of giving, to develop a capacity for love, to untangle the mysteries of sex, to cultivate a competent conscience, to master the management of money, to learn to work and play, to distinguish between fantasy and reality and to achieve in their efforts toward success and happiness. Our ability to help them grow up, to become mature, will mark the measure of our success in preparing them for marriage.

As parents we are imperfect. Our own marriages may be a long way from ideal. We may not show all the characteristics mentioned in the preceding pages. We may be grown up in some respects, but immature in others. We may be strong in some ways, but weak in others. The preceding pages suggest ideals. Ideals are like stars: men have found their way by them all across the ages, but no one has reached one yet.

In the remaining chapters of this book, there is an attempt to spell out more in detail some of the ways in which we help and hinder our children and young people in their growth and development as they prepare for life in general and for marriage in particular. The next chapter deals with our efforts to help them live their own lives.

2

Helping
Them
Live
Their
Own
Lives

WHEN Jerry was born he could breathe, digest, and eliminate. His helplessness was almost complete. His mother had to do everything else for him. As a little human being, his period of growth and development is longer than the young of any other species on earth. He will need a lot of help before he becomes an independent man.

It was a wise providence that planned it so that Jerry's mother had a very strong need to be needed. It was Jerry's helplessness that appealed to her so much. It made her feel very important. She derived a great deal of satisfaction from it. But just as there is no pure happiness, so there is no pure satisfaction. Jerry's mother had other things to do. She was an active member of the Mental Health Board, served on the PTA Council, worked with the other women in her church, and was an officer in the Literary Guild. Jerry interfered.

She was in conflict within herself because she wanted him to remain helpless and yet she wanted him to learn to do things for himself. She wanted these conflicting things both at the same time.

Encouraging Them to Help Themselves

Jerry's mother encouraged him when he began to show signs that he wanted to learn to feed himself, even though it was quite a messy affair. She understood that little ones in the learning process can sneeze with a mouthful of cereal. To a small child nothing seems quite so much fun as turning a cereal bowl upside down on one's head while it is at least half full. We head this off if we see it coming and reprimand if we did not. *However we handle it we make an impression on how Jerry will deal with life, married life included.* It is either an understanding and encouraging world in which a person can get set right, sometimes with firmness, or it is an impatient and sometimes cruel world in which a person can get hurt if he makes a mistake or fails.

Here is a woman who seems utterly helpless around the home. She never can do anything without assistance. When she was a little girl her mother never would let her manage for herself. Her mother did everything for her "because she loved her," she said. Now as a grown woman she cannot succeed at what she undertakes and really does not want to do so because she needs the proof that other people love her which comes from their doing things for her. If she marries a man who wants to be of help to his wife, or who will employ maids to help her, she can be happy. If she gets a man who wants her to stand on her own feet and carry her share of the load he will be angry with her and she will be hurt, if not furious, about it. As parents we must help our children when they really need it, but we must be careful not to do for them what they could do and ought to be doing for themselves.

It is an all too common complaint of wives that they have to pick up after their husbands as if they were little boys. Loving mothers picked up after them right on into manhood. Now a wife has to be a mother to her husband or stir up anger and resentment in demanding that he pick up after himself. Here is one of the small ways in which the Armed Forces may contribute to the further maturation, to the responsible independence, of man-sized boys. In forcing them to take care of their personal belongings the Armed Forces pick up where mother left off, or failed, and play the role of extended mother and father until the boys become men.

In our culture far too many girls never learn how to "keep house." Mother or a maid does everything. The little-girl woman is taught that all she needs to do is look pretty and act attractive. She is made to think that as long as she can look glamorous on a pillow she can marry and live happily ever after. Parents treat her like a living doll. Every husband wants a doll wife, but he wants her to know how to keep the home halfway decent most of the time as well.

Anxiety About Their Decisions

We find it easier to let our children take care of themselves in physical ways because most of the time the risks are not very great and the results can be easily observed. We are much more anxious and tend to be much slower in allowing our children to make their own decisions. We start out making all decisions for them and have to learn to stop. We have had so much more experience and know so much more it seems quite logical for us to continue making their decisions, especially in view of their limited knowledge and lack of experience.

Johnny's mother took him to see the doctor. According to her, Johnny was just plain stubborn. He insisted on doing what she did not want him to do and refused to do what she demanded. The doctor in observing the mother during the interview saw that Johnny had little opportunity to do anything. His mother seemed all over him at every move he made. What she called stubbornness was simply Johnny's last-ditch effort to assert himself. In this instance Johnny's mother was overanxious. She loved him so much and wanted to be such a good mother that she was smother-loving him.

Later, Johnny is very likely going to appear stubborn to some woman who will have consented to be his wife. Whenever she suggests that he do or not do something he may oppose her. He will probably express the feelings of resentment and anger which he could not express toward his mother as a child. His wife may not understand that he is not reacting to her so much as to his childhood mother of whom she reminds him. He may not understand it either.

At least Johnny was asserting himself enough to develop sufficient aggression to be stubborn. Some Johnnies submit completely to this maternal dominance, become "good boys," and never develop enough self-assertion and aggression to succeed as men. They are what the psychologists call "passive submissive" men. They make good husbands for dominant aggressive women except for the inner conflict they have, needing to depend and hating themselves for doing it.

Our Need for Obedience

We need not only to be needed but we need to be respected. With little children obedience means respect. Disobedience means disrespect. Those among us who have been pushed around too much ourselves as children can very easily push our children around in turn because they are too small to resist.

There are many hidden reasons for our need to control. As long as we can control our children they are young and we are young. If and when they arrive at an age where they want to take over control of their own lives, this suggests that we are getting old. Nothing is so threatening to some of us as the idea that we are getting old. We are therefore likely to become more authoritarian than ever and demand obedience with even greater threats of consequences in order to hang on to our own youth. If we hang on too long and demand obedience too constantly we invite rebellion against all authority. There are far too many adults who are still expressing childhood rebellion against any authority symbol they run into.

Jim would have nothing to do with the church, and it nearly broke his wife's heart. His rebellion and rejection were nothing more than reaction to his parents' insistence upon his attendance at church as one means of securing obedience and maintaining control clear through his childhood into his youth until he left home. What looked like marriage conflict was only reaction to childhood experience finding expression in marriage.

Fran was a cute child. Everybody made a fuss over her. She received so much attention that she naturally came to expect it. Everybody gave her presents. Now as a wife and mother she is unhappy if she does not get a similar amount of attention. She cannot get it in her own home. She has joined everything in town, as her husband puts it, and gives more time to community affairs than to her home.

In the community she receives attention. She is lauded and praised for her efforts although she seems more concerned with being considered important than with being liked. At home she is a pessimist. Home is where things go wrong.

Nobody ever thinks of her. She is in a position where she should be thinking of others but she must think of herself first. She was taught to do it by well-meaning, but misguided, parents.

Giving, to her, is a way to secure recognition and appreciation. She does things for members of her family as a kind of social and affectional bribery. She cannot give from love of others. She gives to secure response from others for love of herself. This is immature love in an adult woman. Her parents' indulgence of her made her this way for marriage. She cannot be an adequate mother to her own children.

School—a Step Toward Independence

We all recognize school as a good means of helping in the weaning process. Many of us are glad when our children reach the age when they can go to school. They will no longer be under foot. We recognize that they are growing up in the learning process. We can of course, complicate this by expecting too little or demanding too much of them as far as grades are concerned. A little further along in school it disturbs us if they come home with different ideas from ours. It threatens us if they learn something we do not know. It makes us uneasy if teaching methods change from those with which we are familiar. We may push them too early into the social situation of school dances and dating because we are unsure of ourselves and we want to make sure that they are popular. All children are ego extensions of their parents and they must perform well or their parents are threatened. Parents push hardest at points of their own felt weaknesses.

We are in conflict about it all. If, on the first day of school, when we leave Junior he trots off and immediately begins to play quite happily with the other children, we are hurt because we wanted him to be reluctant to leave us. That would inflate our ego and make us feel good. If he hangs on and whines or cries, and doesn't want to be turned loose and go with the other children, we are flattered. At the same time we are worried because we feel he should go play with the others. We do not want a cry baby and we want him to be able to hold his own with the other children.

On the way home we feel greatly relieved to realize that he will not be around for a while. Then suddenly we feel terribly guilty for feeling relieved. All this is quite normal. Only when we go to some extreme with respect to it, are we likely to threaten our own children. Leave us they must, and the process is painful all along the way.

Suddenly we realize that school will be over. What if we are not there and miss him, and he has to walk home by himself? There are several streets to be crossed. There is a lot of traffic. There are dogs along the way. There are bigger children who might pick on him—and we become frightened. We want guarantees of his safety. But even if we could have guarantees it would not be good for him. We may accompany him for the first few days, but sooner or later he must learn to find his way home in the larger world outside. We have to stand the strain of the risks. We have to face the pain of tragic possibilities in order to allow for the development of his independence.

Our Anxiety for Their Social Success

One of the chief reasons for too young marriage is over-anxiety on the part of mothers about the social acceptability of their daughters. Parents are so afraid that their children will not be popular that they push them into social situations too early and dress them like little sex objects with apparently no understanding of possible consequences. Many times there is more concern for popularity on the part of mothers than on the part of the children themselves. We may push them because we are unsure of ourselves and we want to make sure that they are popular.

Under such circumstances children are denied the normal process of growing up and the fun of childhood years. They are forced into situations where they must become "little adults" long before they arrive near adulthood. Far too many married people are now restless and they respond to attractions outside marriage because of the feeling that they missed a lot in the growing-up years. They now want to catch up on the side, and this frequently leads to trouble. Because of our own anxieties, we can push our children into a distorted growth and development which will affect their marriage relationships later.

The Dating Daze

When our young people begin to date we can show our confidence in them. We can support them by listening to their expressions of concern and by arriving at joint decisions about such matters as how many dates a week, how late they may stay out, whom they go with, and where they go. When we assume the role of dictator we are asking for rebellion and the kind of sneaking around that some young people are forced to do. If we are too unconcerned or if we thrust too much responsibility upon them, they can get over their depth in trouble which may be of our making.

For parents there are no simple solutions, ten easy lessons, or pat answers. But we encourage and support, or we threaten and alienate according to the way we deal with them during these years. The important thing seems to be merely being close enough to listen to their anxieties and their triumphs, to offer suggestions or express understand-

ing, to communicate our concern and affection. Hundreds
of young people, when speaking of their parents to a personal counselor in one connection or another, complain,
"They never listen to me." "I have had absolutely no help
in trying to understand myself." "We are never together
alone so that we could talk." "I know my father loves me.
I wish I knew him."

When an adolescent is smitten with infatuation a parent
may react in anxiety. Some parents panic, others pray. What
we are afraid of is sex. Whether we have reason to be afraid
depends to a great degree on how adequately we have con-
ducted their sex education from early childhood. If this
represents a chasm between us we may have some reason
to be anxious. If we have discussed the story of life and made
it possible for our children and young people to read books
on sex education suitable to their age in efforts to understand
themselves and others better, we may be much more confident while the turbulent experiences of young love are
going on.

We may be afraid of sex in their lives because of what
happened to us in our youth. Many of us, in looking back,
decide that we were too careless, and so we wish to be very
careful with our children. We conclude that we were too
ignorant or too wild, and so we clamp down. Here, as in
all other respects, our own childhood and youth influence
the treatment of our children. If we can get our own past
into proper perspective, our own emotions into some balance, we may be able to talk with our children and young
people as they want and need us to communicate. If we can
help them to form a value system that requires respect for
persons as ends and not merely means to selfish ends we may
be more relaxed. If we can help them to develop a firm faith
and a strong conscience we may trust them.

Threats of Young Marriage

In some instances early marriage means that our young people are trying to get away from us. Marriage looks like an escape route. Either we are too unconcerned about them, we never listen to them, and don't seem to care what happens to them, or we are overconcerned about them and we order their lives in a manner that we consider safe, regardless of their feelings. We deny them the development of their own selves and any independent responsibility. Most of the time desire for escape emerges out of neglect or dominance.

Sometimes youngsters jump into too early marriage because of failure or fear of failure. If we set too high goals or press them too hard for achievement or if we have not been sufficiently encouraging to give them confidence in themselves they may try to avoid the showdown by quitting. These kinds of feelings and attitudes that children and young people can get as a result of the way we deal with them, go with them right on into marriage and have much to do with their success or failure in it.

A young couple, not yet out of high school, were drawn to each other out of a common need. Their relationship became intimate and soon a baby was on the way. They ran off and were secretly married. They came from homes where little or no love was expressed. Each was starving for affection. It was one of thousands of forced marriages caused by unintended pregnancy. It is no solution to condemn the couple for violating the moralities. Their parents had violated their moral responsibility to supply adequate attention and affection long years before.

Perhaps the parents were too busy. Perhaps they thought giving their children money, clothes, and things asked for was enough. More tragically, perhaps they could not love or could not express their love and had to give material things to try to make up for it. Not all parents can love as their children need. Some parents are victims of their own parents' inadequacy and incompetency. What matters here is that we realize that we are shaping our children's marriages by the way we deal with them as children.

We should not blame all premarital pregnancies and forced marriages on the failure of parents to provide adequate affection, or discipline, or sex education, or to teach a high moral standard. Research from the fields of psychology and sociology points to many other influences playing upon our children as they grow up. But some people have gone off the deep end pointing toward society or family and holding delinquent youth blameless. Some such youths have been quick to exploit the idea when their delinquency was the result of deliberate disregard of responsibility.

It is true that social pressure on some of our college campuses, just like social pressures in our own communities, have gotten people into trouble even when there was plenty of affection at home. But total responsibility cannot be placed upon social pressure since all of us have developed whatever resistance we have to it and are responsible to exercise it. Another way to say that social pressure is too strong is to say that we are too weak. In any case for all of us, parents have had and do have something to do with the development of resistance to social pressure.

From the arrival of our children at puberty on through the teens, all of us as parents have the problem of accepting the rejection with which our children confront us. The fact that our own children seem to accept any other adult as more of an authority than we are on anything can hurt our feelings. If we understand this as characteristic of the reach for independence, we can welcome it as a sign of their increasing maturity. If we do not understand it, then our ego can be greatly hurt and we can interfere in the growth process or damage it by our jealous reactions.

It helps if we remember what our children are up against. As young people they are having to develop new and more mature relationships with their friends of the same age. What their friends think and feel becomes very important. As parents we shall need to take a different attitude toward their friends too. We reassure them when we treat them as nearing adulthood. We threaten when we act toward them as if they were still children.

Some of us found it much easier to figure out what it means to be "masculine" or "feminine." What makes a man a man, or a woman a woman, was more clearly defined when we were young. Now it is all mixed up. It is confusing to us unless we hang on to the old stereotypes. It is more confusing to our children if we do. The old images are changing. They have to find out what becoming a man and being masculine, or becoming a woman and being feminine, means in this space age.

As their bodies change from childhood shape to the physical maturity of manhood and womanhood they may become self-conscious. We may help them accept the changes and feel proud of them or we may make them even more self-conscious and embarrassed by teasing or by attempts to be humorous. Much will depend upon how we feel and think about our own bodies. Most of us know very little about the wonderful construction and function of the most intricate, complex example of machine automation in the universe. We take our bodies for granted. If we have respect and admiration for our bodies with more than the usual superficial knowledge and self-conscious embarrassment about them, our children may be helped to accept and respect their physical growth and development. If we are emotionally inhibited and ignorant we may block our children from a healthy understanding or force them elsewhere for it.

If we can realize that any young person who is restless and confused, who is impatient and emotionally unstable, who alternates between lethargy and enthusiasm, laziness and noisy activity, who is forgetful and inconsistent *is a normal young person*, we may come nearer to accepting our own children when they are that way. If we can see that their desire for independence is in conflict with their need to depend, that their demand for privilege is out of gear with their responsibility, that their behavior falls far short of their own high ideals, and that they can fall in love at the drop of a schoolbook—if we can *recognize all this as characteristic* of *youth's struggle to grow up*, we may be of more help to our children.

In the very midst of adolescent turbulence our older children show a seriousness about life that should give us confidence in them and cause us to show it. That is what they need —namely, the reassurance of our confidence. They are aware that they may someday marry and are full of anxieties as well as romantic illusions about it. They want to find the right mate and make a success of the establishment of their own homes. When our older children begin to talk of marriage we feel they are too young.

We can support the high school in providing opportunity in the curriculum for our young people to see what has been found out about marriage through research. We can support any move to provide the best books on preparation for marriage which can be secured for the school and public libraries. We can support the church in its efforts to help through group discussions, engaged-couple lectures, and the minister's premarital counseling.

It helps if we can understand that at the same time that we are confronted with turning our children loose, they are confronted with their lingering desire to hang on. They want to be free, but they cannot quite let go. This is as much a dilemma for them as it is for us. What matters is that they gain their freedom and that we discover ours too. It is the kind of freedom that comes with the gradual shift of responsibility. If that is not accomplished they will never be able to deal effectively with the problems of adult life, especially marriage.

Betty was forever talking about her father. Her husband was fed up with it. He felt that Betty considered her parents superior to his. She consulted her father before agreeing to anything she and her husband had to decide. Her father, in his ignorance, was flattered by this continuing consultation by his daughter. He felt that he was making a real contribution to her marriage. It was instead a contribution which almost broke it up.

Betty's husband realized soon after marriage that he would have trouble with his wife's parents, especially her father. It was not that Betty's father actually butted in or tried to make decisions for them, but that her husband tried to get Betty to assume responsibility for her own thinking and feelings and leave her dad out of it. She was so resistant that it looked as if she were the victim of a too close attachment to her father. Her husband consulted a marriage counselor about the situation and persuaded Betty to come later for an interview.

After several sessions with them and with Betty's father things began to change. When Betty realized that she had taken her husband's hand and had never really let go of her father's, she determined to act more like a wife and less like a little girl. Her father helped by refusing to tell her what to do. A great deal of struggle could have been avoided if he had refused earlier.

Mothers can help or hinder very much. Remember the story of the mother who was telling her friends about her children's marriages? Her daughter was extremely fortunate. Her husband did the dishes and a lot of the housework even though there were no children yet. He was a wonderful husband. He even served his wife's breakfast in bed. But her son had been extremely unfortunate. He had married a girl who was so helpless he had to do the dishes and most of the housework, and the selfish little witch wanted him to serve her breakfast in bed!

We need to help our children learn how to paddle their own canoes. They need us for a while in the canoe to offer suggestions and encouragement and to help them keep it from turning over. But someday we must get out of the canoe and hand them the paddle. We show our confidence in our parenthood in trusting them. If we cannot trust them it is a confession of fear of our own failure as parents.

If we are successful as parents we make ourselves useless as parents. The purpose of parenthood is to work ourselves out of a job. If we understand this and accomplish it fairly well, we can have a very real sense of pride in our own achievement and in the responsible independence of our children. They leave us as children and return to us as capable young adults.

Too frequently affectional ties are strained or broken in this final weaning process. If things go well, we discover a new affectionate regard for each other on a much more mature level. In early childhood respect may be demonstrated by obedience; but, as children grow into young adults, respect on our part is demonstrated by our confidence that they can deal with life adequately on their own. This is the kind of respect that we all want and need from others. It is the kind of respect our grown children need from us. The more help we are to our children in their efforts to learn to live their own lives across the years of childhood and youth, the more adequately we help them to prepare for their own marriage.

3

Easing Their Struggles with Rules and Regulations

W HAT DOES a child's struggle with rules and regulations have to do with its marriage later? We are confronted with rules and regulations all through life. Marriage is no exception. There are the hard, fixed rules called laws. Every state has laws governing marriage. There are the more fluid yet very real rules and regulations of custom and tradition. There are the soft yet perhaps more real and vital rules and regulations of commitments, promises, and love. The attitude we develop toward them through childhood and youth builds integrity or a lack of it. There is no substitute for it in marriage.

50

Obedience Is Necessary

Children must learn to obey. They must learn it early for the sake of their survival and welfare. Jimmy has no idea about automobiles and the dangers in the street. Jimmy's mother or daddy or anyone else around who is older and understands about streets has the responsibility of making Jimmy obey when they say, "Stay out of the street." Disobedience under these circumstances could be harmful if not fatal. Later, Jimmy is going to promise to keep himself only to his wife. Disobedience could be very harmful if not fatal to his marriage.

Frances had to be made to stay away from the stove when pots with hot liquids in them were at the scalding stage. Frances did not know about fire or hot water, so mother or somebody else had to make Frances obey. Disobedience under these circumstances could result in terrible consequences. There are no ifs, ands, or buts about it. When life or safety is involved obedience is necessary, and parents must have it from their children.

Too often we read in the papers about some child who has died because it did not obey its parents. Sometimes it dies because parents do not enforce obedience. In some instances parents are unable to face their responsibility for the consequences. They rationalize in self-defense, asserting that "God took the dear, sweet, young thing in order to save it from some terrible tragedy later in life" or because "it was too pure and innocent for this world."

Whether you consider the Ten Commandments a statement of high ideals or recognize them as the lowest common denominator upon which any group can survive, you will find among them the admonition to children that they obey their parents. Here is religious authority for our expecting it and demanding it. Whether the principle is God-given or a matter of necessity as a result of the blood, sweat, and tears through the accumulated experience of the human race, apparently it remains a sound principle.

Whatever the relation of obedience to our child's safety and survival, it is necessary for *our* feeling of responsibility and importance. Our attitudes and feelings about the obedience of our children are all tangled up with the way *we* have grown and developed across the years. If we have grown up, constructed a strong ego, and feel reasonably safe in the world we shall require obedience for the sake of our children. If we are immature and driven by a weak ego, we are likely to overdo the feeling that it is a very unsafe and insecure world and demand obedience for our own sake. Obedience, like any other virtue, is necessary for human welfare; but it can be pushed to such an extreme that it may defeat our purpose.

Rules Are Necessary

Rules and regulations are necessary, but we may have too few or too many. We could be too lax or inconsistent with their enforcement, or too harsh in our demand and treatment. Children in finding themselves and asserting themselves are going to run afoul of rules. If we push them too hard they can become lazy or stubborn. They could become rebellious and fight back. If we know how to read the signs, if we understand what our children's behavior means, we can help them.

No child can be fenced with rules without being angry when he runs into the fences. He is frustrated and made anxious and he is bound to express it. Usually the expression is noisy if not violent, accompanied by looks and acts of anger, if not hatred, directed toward his parents. This is too much for unstable and insecure parents. They cannot stand the possibility of their child not liking them, and so they give in. They cannot say "No," even when they know they should say "No!" and make it stick!

Such research as we have suggests that much adult hostility and guilt has roots in family life where parents were severely autocratic. Severe autocracy in parenthood is frequently coupled with lack of trust. Inability to trust is a reflection of a feeling of one's own untrustworthiness. On the other hand, much friendliness and spontaneity in adults seems to have a background of democratic family attitudes where discipline was firm but not harsh, where parents could and did trust each other and their children.

Strong parents understand that anxiety, frustration, and inner conflict are inevitable for children whenever they run up against rules. These parents are prepared to accept their children's reactions as characteristic of the learning process. They permit them an expression of their frustration and accept their momentary demonstration of anger and hostility without themselves being too threatened or upset by it. They can remain firm without melting or freezing before their child's hostility. The way parents handle their children in moments like this, shapes and conditions the way the children will respond to authority later in life and to discipline in marriage. It conditions how they will treat their own children.

Immature Adults Fear the Law

Not long ago I was talking with a prominent judge. He remarked that a great many people who were brought before him reminded him of little boys or little girls caught in some misdemeanor by their parent. Their attitude toward him was precisely the attitude of a child toward a parent in such circumstances. As a result of this conversation I began to observe the attitude and feeling of people about the law and those who are charged with enforcing it.

It has been amusing to observe the behavior of many of my friends in the presence of an officer. They suddenly become very careful and very much on their good behavior. They act just like a child in the presence of a disciplining parent. The minute the father-image in the police uniform disappears they become relaxed and can be themselves again. Frequently the comments they make with reference to the officer reflect the defiance and rebellion which characterize childhood. Those of my friends who have grown up seem to change least in the presence of a policeman or in being reminded of law.

A great many adults display attitudes toward the law very similar to children's attitudes toward rules and regulations. Either they proceed in open defiance and feel that they gain some kind of status because of it, or they submit docilely in fear of punishment. They carry such childish resentment of authority that they will gang up on an enforcing officer in the discharge of the duty for which they employed him. Open defiance of law and the enforcing officer, on the part of older young people and adults, strongly suggests parental failure. If parents mishandle authority and discipline, children can become resentful and defiant of any reminder of authority or discipline. The roots of order and security for any culture are enmeshed in childhood experiences. Security in marriage has the same roots.

One way in which the pioneer mother was known as a good mother or a bad mother was by whether she could go outside and hang out clothes without taking all the children with her. Early pioneer homes had dirt floors and open fireplaces. If she was the authority and protection for her children, the authority and protection went out with her when she left the cabin. She had to take the children with her to be sure of their safety. If she had striven to transfer the authority and protection to the children themselves, she might risk going outside and leaving them alone in the house.

It is painful to watch a child fascinated with the attraction of a glowing coal on the hearth advance and touch it. But it may be a means of establishing an understanding of the nature of fire that would transfer authority and protection from the parent to the child itself with reference to an open fireplace. Far too many of us are not willing to stand the pain of helping our children to learn. We attempt to do it altogether by telling them. We love them and do not want them to have to learn the hard way, and so we try to give them the benefit of our experience. To a small degree this works, but each generation seems to have to learn some things for itself. Better a singed finger than third-degree burns over the body.

When our children reach the years of adolescence they become naturally more self-assertive. They want to assume responsibility for the living of their own lives. This means they want authority and they want to discipline themselves. If we have been too slow in allowing them to have authority they may break away in open rebellion. As previously pointed out, many a running jump into young marriage is for no other reason so much as to escape parental dominance.

Defiance and rebellion may break out in their marriage later, triggered by husband or wife attitudes or actions which unconsciously remind them of our misuse of authority as parents when they were children. When we overdo authority they may overdo it in turn in dealing with their children years later, because of an unconscious desire for revenge!

If children submit docilely to our continued authority and discipline they may become so dependent that they cannot stand on their own feet. They remain tied to us and will have to lean on us straight on into the adult years. Here are roots for in-law troubles and much unhappiness in marriage. When boys accept our authority and discipline passively, research suggests that they may not be able to compete very well as men among men and with regard to masculine interests. Passivity seems to be associated with sexual anxiety and the need to prove adequacy through premarital sexual activity. It could result in impotency in marriage.

We Must Transfer Discipline

It is not possible for us to relinquish authority and transfer responsibility for discipline from ourselves to our children without risks, both to our feelings of satisfaction and security, and to their welfare. If we love them and are very greatly concerned we cannot accomplish this without considerable anxiety. But accomplish it we must.

I remember the father whose high school son had been agitating for some time for the right to establish his own rules about how many dates a week and what time he would come in at night. The father made it plain that responsibility went along with rights. He agreed to a trial period, but indicated that he would examine his son's grade reports at the end of the period to see how they might reflect his success or failure. He advised his son that he would make as one condition a physical check with the family doctor immediately and again at the same time that he looked at his grade reports.

The father, in talking with me, stated that his main purpose was to help his son realize what rules and regulations were all about. He wanted his son to check at least two ways to tell whether he was being successful. Loss of sleep and unwise eating habits would show up as a consequence in his physical health and in his achievement scores at school.

His son did a fair job for a while then began to let down. The father and mother saw it but left decision to him. Once, under pressure from his friends when he really wanted to say no, be begged his mother not to let him go. She helped him out of it so that he could shift to her the responsibility for the rule and for his obeying it. When his father found out he was angry with both his son and his wife. He wanted an all-or-nothing arrangement, but they ended with a compromise. There are times when a son or daughter needs parental rules and authority to fall back on.

Sometimes a young person is too unsure of himself to venture on his own and needs a little push from his parents. One spring I watched a mother wren encouraging her young to fly. She fluttered about and chattered advice as each little bird floundered up to the edge of the nest and looked over into the great depths, cluttered by branches, between it and the ground. One little bird took off as soon as he reached the edge of the nest. It was a poor job of flying, and he looked both surprised and offended after he picked himself up off the ground. It was obvious that he still had a lot to learn before he could fly with grace and safety.

Other little wrens followed one by one as they considered the situation and made the great adventure. One little bird, however, squawked and chirped around the edge of the nest, jumping back into the middle of it, instead of out of it. The mother bird continued to offer advice. I thought I detected a note of irritation in her voice. I was sure of it in a few moments when she flew straight to the nest, jumped down into the middle of it and proceeded to push the little one out. There was no hesitation on her part.

Perhaps it was knowledge supplied by the Creator. The mother wren seemed to understand that unless her little one got out of that nest and struggled to develop its own wings it would never fly. Instinctively, she knew she could not fly for it. The days of her protecting it were over. She would continue to help with advice and warnings, but sooner or later the little bird would be on its own. It was time for it to develop its own wings.

In observing friends across the years, we have all seen overanxious parents push their children out of the nest too soon. If their anxiety went in the other direction they stood on the edge of the nest and pushed them back into it when the little ones wanted to try their own wings. The decision when to push and when to hold back is not a matter of instinct with us. For too many it seems to be tradition or some pattern we call "common sense" which is a kind of rationalizing term for our own opinion. It should rest upon a sensitive awareness of the level of maturation of our child. This presupposes enough knowledge and perception to recognize the signs when we see them.

Rules and decisions based upon them should be understood by parents and children. With the little ones explanation and discussion are of little avail. As our children grow they may understand more easily and come to participate in the establishment of whatever rules and regulations relate to them in the home. They may be able to accept and abide by them in the main, but they may need the strength of our enforcement on occasion. Here are roots for how they will accept and abide by promises they make later at a wedding.

Over the years we have observed thousands of students in college. We have seen reflections of their attitudes in their behavior toward rules and regulations. We have seen the docilely submissive and the openly rebellious. Both have concerned us. Such attitudes reflect parental floundering in helping them to understand the nature and meaning of rules and to achieve some ability to adjust to them. Some students seem quite naturally to understand their significance; and when and if they feel that any rule or regulation is out of line or not essential any more, they go through procedures established for its change or its elimination. Their maturity in comparison with the other students is quite obvious.

Some years ago a group of men students at a university made a panty raid on one of the dormitories for women. It spread to other dorms. More students joined the crowd. It was not long before men who were not students joined and by that time the gathering was a mob. It began to destroy property. It moved from the university to the campuses of the two women's colleges in town. Before it was disbursed nearly a hundred thousand dollars in damage had been done.

There were plenty of rules and regulations. The willingness and the ability to abide by them was missing. Personal authority in terms of self-discipline broke down. There were laws but not enough officers to enforce them. The result was mob violence and destruction of property.

I have often wondered what might have happened if regard for those rules and regulations established for the safety of *persons* had been ignored. Our children have a right to a clear understanding of the relation of rules, regulations, and laws to our freedom and security. We fail unless we make sure that our children see that relationship. If they want the right to relate themselves directly to the rules and laws, they must understand their responsibility and we must hold them responsible. Our attitude will have considerable influence in this matter.

There are rules, regulations, moralities, and laws involved in marriage. Husbands or wives may cheat, deceive, defy, ignore, or openly violate depending partly upon attitudes and feelings about such rules and regulations which reflect parental treatment and childhood response. Adultery and other forms of infidelity may demonstrate little regard for rules, regulations, morality, and law. Where our own attitude toward rules is characterized by regard and respect our children are more likely to acquire the same attitude.

An account appeared in a newspaper telling of a father who had violated some traffic regulation and been given a ticket by the arresting police officer. His son was with him. The father fumed all the way home, vowing that he would get the matter fixed by friends at city hall and give the officer "a hard way to go" because of it. After he cooled off he began to realize what his performance was teaching his son. The next day he called the boy to him and explained how a person says things in anger that he doesn't really mean. He then took his son with him to court, pleaded guilty, and paid his fine. On the way home he talked with his son about the relation of traffic laws to safety. That is hardheaded, good sense and realistic parenthood. The boy was lucky to have a dad like that. He will more likely make a good husband and better father.

Our Power Struggles Have Roots

Frequently a woman in her attitude and behavior toward her husband is simply rebelling against and punishing her father. She has never been helped to understand and adjust to authority. Rules and regulations which spell it out create hostility in her. Any time her husband unconsciously reminds her of her father, she reacts to him as she had wanted to react to her father when she was a little girl. Many a husband carries the overload of his wife's reaction to her childhood relation to her father. It seems quite unfair and all out of proportion in the husband-wife relationship.

The same thing can happen as far as a man is concerned. His relations with his wife involve childhood relations to his mother. Some husbands in dealing with their wives are rebelling against or punishing their mothers. The way we deal with our children across the years is directly related to how they will get along with their husband or wife when they are married.

Fortunately it works both ways. Some wives, in dealing with their husbands, are paying a very high tribute to their fathers. Many a young husband owes a very great deal to his wife's father for the manner in which he helped her to trust and to express her love and affection. Similarly, many a wife owes much to her husband's mother who is responsible to a great degree for his capacity to love her and to respond to her according to her needs.

In dealing with our children we reveal the nature of our own childhood experience with our parents. If we were too browbeaten the chances are we shall browbeat our own children, partially to take revenge and partially to prove that we can now dominate where then we had to submit. This kind of experience is behind many a parent's determination to show a husband or wife and the children who is boss.

Our struggles in marriage are a reflection of our needs for respect and security. If we need to prove something, control of others is reassuring. Much parental dominance is motivated by parental insecurity. Since all parents are insecure to some extent, there is nothing abnormal about this until it becomes extreme. The abnormality is revealed by the extremity.

A complicating factor in our day is the changing roles of woman. In family life patterned after the patriarchal form the father was the dominant figure, the authority, the head of the house, the disciplinarian. The mother was his helpmeet, subservient to him and responsible for the training of the children. In today's world where women have invaded man's realm and compete with him in the world outside the home and expect men to share work with them in the home, the power struggle between husband and wife is perhaps more prevalent than ever before. Children frequently become the battleground for this power struggle. Young people approaching the age for marriage may be caught in the middle where parents compete for authority in applying rules for adolescent behavior. How we manage this struggle between ourselves from the birth of our babies until they are grown and gone from home will have a great deal to do with how they behave in their own marriages.

Whatever the principles and policies in our family, we can be sure that they are not quite the same in families of our children's friends. Our children are exposed to these differences. Their problem of deciding and developing confidence in their own decisions in the face of perhaps a greater period of confusion than in any other time in history, is indeed a great one. Help is available to a few of them in school in terms of courses providing insight into the maturation process. In some schools there are courses dealing with family life and education for marriage. Help may be available after they are married in terms of marriage counseling. These were not available to us. Even with this help they are not going to have an easy time of it. If we have done our best to help them in their struggle with rules and regulations, they are likely to have a much happier marriage and be more competent parents. They will be more responsible citizens.

We turn now to examine the emerging self-consciousness of our children and our relation as parents to it. In all relationships the way we think of ourselves and the way we feel about ourselves is very important. In marriage relationships it is critical.

4

Stimulating
Their
Discovery
of
Themselves

THE UNITED STATES has been called a country of status
seekers. Books have been published about it. Much is
made of various status symbols. It would appear that there
are a great many adults in our country who are very badly
in need of the feeling of amounting to something.

The Real Meaning of "Status Seekers"

Status is a word that stands for what we think of ourselves
and how we feel about ourselves. This self-image determines
how we regard ourselves. The more inferior we think ourselves to be, or feel that we are, the stronger the desire and
the drive for status. Some people marry for status. Some
build homes to show off to their friends and neighbors. Some
drive automobiles purchased for the specific purpose of im-
pressing people. When we were in Europe not long ago we
noticed, particularly in England, that an overwhelming ma-

jority of the cars were old. My son made the observation that English people must think of cars as a means of transportation. His implication was clear.

The symbols change. Perhaps a later symbol is the boat. If you can drag a boat behind your car it does not make so much difference about the car. The symbols vary among the professions and the businesses. Offices with windows are higher in status value than those without; two windows are higher than one; offices with rugs, higher than those with other types of floor covering; cars with telephones can snub those without.

It all goes back to the early years of childhood. Children depend on the attitudes of the adults around them for how they think and feel about themselves. Those adults closest to them and dearest to them have the most influence. If we, in dealing with our children, supply them with enough approval and praise for their accomplishments, their need for reassurance is more nearly satisfied. They can develop self-confidence and self-regard. If we love them and show this love in our affectionate dealing with them, their image of themselves and feeling about themselves is satisfying.

Development of the Self

The most important thing about any of us is the self. It is growing and developing and being shaped importantly by parents all through the childhood years. When parents are too busy with business or social life, or when parents are too harsh in their disciplining or when they tend to ignore the children, the question arises in the mind of a child, "What's wrong with me?" Doubts regarding worthfulness and acceptability are planted. Sometimes our reactions to children's efforts to reassure themselves only create greater anxiety and doubt in them.

Above everything else children must be loved. Attention may mean that they are. If children are not sure that they are loved, they strive harder to get attention. If they cannot get it through approved behavior, they will get it through disapproved behavior. Attention that carries punishment with it is better than no attention at all. Punishment suggests to the child that at least parents care that much anyway.

Did you ever notice how a child that is approved and praised for some achievement seems to unfold and extend himself and venture into more and better achievement? The child confronted with criticism and condemnation or with the most vicious weapon anyone can use against a child—ridicule—withdraws within himself, shrinks up, and quits trying. A great amount of rule breaking and the destruction of property, called delinquency, is due to the fact that such youths were never given adequate assurance of their own worthfulness and acceptability.

The real importance of parents' night at school is not the money made for the PTA. It is the support given each child by parents who come to see what their child has done and to praise it. The child is proud if parents are proud. Parents can keep motivation alive and healthy by such recognition and encouragement. They keep self-confidence growing in their child.

I knew a man who on parents' night gave proud attention to the achievements of his children until they were satisfied. He then went from room to room to find children whose parents did not come. He would inquire about such a child's displays, insist that they be pointed out to him and comment on what fine pieces of work they were. It is almost pathetic to watch children's eyes, dull with disappointment, light up because of such recognition and appreciation. It is heartwarming to see a face, set to hide loneliness and hurt, become animated at a little really sincere attention. It is the self that is reflected in the achievement; and, in recognizing and appreciating the achievement, we nourish the little self.

Some parents rationalize that they are too busy. Some are not interested. Either they do not realize what their absence can do to their child's feelings about himself—or they do not care. Young people with such parents are likely to start dating early and cling to each other, hanging on to the attention and support they get from each other which they cannot get at home. They are likely to be forced into early marriage. Some do not find anyone to cling to and they grope through youth into adulthood convinced that they are not worth loving, much less marrying.

Damage with Intent to Help

We as parents have to learn how to help our children distinguish between our disapproval of them and our disapproval of something they have done. They must have the assurance that we love them and can be depended on to continue loving them regardless of what they do. When love is used to compel behavior, it is a misuse of food desperately needed by the hungry little self for its growth and development.

There are times when we have a difficult task in dealing with our children to convince them of our fairness. Their individual differences, because of unique personalities, require different treatment on our part. We have all observed that one child needs more attention than another, one child needs more affection than another, and one child needs more discipline than another. In any event, the important thing in dealing with our children is to remember the developing self. On the strength of this self will depend much success and happiness through the adult years in marriage and out of it.

Modern training for elementary-school teachers includes

the information that each child needs to be successful in something and perhaps superior to all its age mates in at least one thing. Teachers, therefore, try hard to discover the various abilities and potentialities of each child as an individual. They tend to encourage achievement whenever they find an ability or an aptitude that shows promise. Their response to achievement is such as to feed the child's needs for recognition, acceptance, and regard.

We know that the teacher who likes teaching, who likes himself or herself in the teaching process gives children the impression that they are liked too. The teacher who is enthusiastic attracts and impresses. Such a teacher is perhaps the greatest influence in the learning process. The same principles seem to hold for us who are parents. If we like being parents, if we like ourselves as parents, if we are enthusiastic about our family life, our children thrive and grow. We do not have to feel this way all the time, just most of the time. We do not have to be perfect, but we need to be headed that way. Our children, as they grow, will permit us to be human. They may love us more for it. Perhaps it is a wise providence that gives children imperfect parents to help them get ready for an imperfect world.

There is no need to evade facing the child with the reality of his own situation when compared to the abilities of other students. There are differences. We are neither honest nor kind if we do not help him to understand this. Sooner or later he will realize that this difference is one of the realities in life. At first the great need is simply reassurance that he is an acceptable, worthful, competent, and adequate little self.

The strongest struggle for self-esteem comes in the latter part of the grades and in early high school in the form of extreme competitiveness. Those who are best at the physical expression of themselves get their sense of status from being athletes; the musician from playing in the band; the actor, from his participation in dramatics. The student achieves status from his straight A's; the football queen, from her personal appearance and social popularity. Too much pressure about athletics, extra class participation or grades can establish expectations beyond a child's ability to achieve and doom the child to failure and despair. Not enough pressure may imply a lack of parental belief that the child can accomplish much, or suggest that we do not care and therefore cause hesitancy or lack of any real effort to achieve.

Sensing a child's needs for support and encouragement, without providing too much or too little, is not easy. Some parents put pressure on a child according to their own need —not the child's need. They are not reacting to the child, but to themselves. Their own self-consciousness about grades and their oversensitivity to what others might think is more influential than what their child needs or how it feels.

One of the problems of counselors in the school system is to recognize the specific achievements of those with talents and ability and to encourage developments of other areas which may have been neglected because they did not do well or receive recognition in them. Education includes the development of resources of the whole person and should prevent the distortion of extreme development of one capacity or ability at the expense of all the others. Such persons are not good marriage material. They are too limited and one-sided.

A personal counselor may well be concerned about his straight A students and those who make F. It might be that the straight A student is brilliant. It could also be that the straight A student is putting all efforts into study to compensate for inadequacy and failure in social life. In any event, it is a revelation of the need of the self for recognition and appreciation which, in this case, is secured through making good grades. In the case of the student who makes F, it could be a lack of ability. Very frequently it is due to the fear of failure. Guilt and the need for self-punishment or the unconscious desire to punish parents is behind many a failure in school. It could be the reason for failure in business, or vocation, or in marriage, for that matter.

A Meaning of Shyness

The shy boys or girls are those who are so unsure of themselves that they will not venture into any situation where what they are afraid of might be proved. Rather than face a showdown, they will simply stay out of it. Shyness may mean inferiority feeling or at least a sense of inadequacy. The situation is too important for them to have this lack revealed. Therefore, they linger around the wall at the dance or go outside and make noise. Frequently this fear of the self, inadequate confidence in the self, the belief that the self is not good enough or does not have ability will be misinterpreted by parents and other adults as lack of ambition. It is nearly always closely associated with poor achievement. The self-image and self-regard are the key to understanding in much of the personal counseling done with both young people and adults. They are involved in premarital and marriage counseling too.

The Influence of Dating

When our youngsters arrive at puberty, and the chemical changes in their bodies influencing psychological and emotional attitudes push them across the sex line to a new consciousness of their own and the opposite sex, it becomes very important for them to learn to swim in the social sea. Popularity becomes a priority. Popularity means that I am "O.K.", I am all right. I am acceptable, a likeable, desirable, worthful person. The need to feel this way is behind any strong drive for popularity. It can be a very great need. Because of inadequate parental supply in the earlier childhood years, a boy or girl can be desperate enough to engage in behavior that is personally threatening or socially dangerous in order to get it. It can threaten any marriage.

The powerful negative influence of "chicken" is tied directly to the need for acceptance and esteem. The weaker the self, the more powerful the threat of being considered afraid. The term "chicken" or whatever term, depending on which generation coins it, means "being looked down on." The desperate effort to prove even at the risk of life, that one is not afraid is really a pitiable confession of weakness and a tragic attempt to prove strength. It is precisely the same cluster of feelings as that which drives the bully. At bottom it is a hunger to be regarded and accepted as a worthful self.

Being invited to join clubs and organizations or achieving membership in them is very important because it tends to prove what the self is most concerned about—namely, that it be an acceptable self. With the arrival of adolescence, age mates take on a new importance. In these years of life, being accepted and regarded by them may be as important—perhaps more important—than being accepted and regarded by one's own parents.

The young are still dependent to a great measure upon what others think of them for how they think and feel about themselves. They have begun to be conscious of self-awareness and self-regard. This is not yet strong enough to stand on its own and therefore the need for approval, for respect, for admiration and regard from their fellows.

Where love is experienced and fades out, and is experienced again several times, the self is repeatedly threatened and reassured. Not just one, but several persons, among age mates have proved the worthfulness and attractiveness, the desirability and acceptability of the loved one. Some young people are tremendously attracted to a certain person as long as they are not sure that they could make the person respond to them. Just as soon as they get the other one interested they lose their own interest. This attraction was only a compulsion to prove their own attractiveness. When proved there are no further grounds for the relationship. The person looks for new fields to conquer. This accounts for much flirting in marriage, or rather flirting out of marriage. It could lead to illicit affairs. The basic cause is the same, the need for reassurance regarding the attractiveness and acceptability of the self.

The young person most unsure of himself, or herself, is most likely to fall in love first and to fall hardest. The greater the need for reassurance the greater the fall when infatuation does occur. For anyone to feel that way about me and take the attitudes which that feeling causes them to take toward me, is final and absolute proof of my acceptance among my age mates. It proves my likeability and worthfulness to a point of being deserving of love. This is one of the reasons why early love is so satisfying. It meets perhaps the greatest need we have for reassurance with respect to ourselves.

This might also explain why, for those who are less sure of themselves, holding on to love is a matter of desperation when and if it seems that it might fade out or someone else might take it away. The extreme jealousy that characterizes early young love is really fear of losing possession of the loved one and anger toward any real or supposed threat. The important thing is that the young person needs love so desperately as proof of his own desirability and worthfulness. Any threat of loss of love is a direct threat to the idea of adequacy of the self and regard for the self. Efforts to maintain the love are "self"-defensive measures.

Young people can become so desperate about it that they threaten harm to themselves or others unless the love is maintained. It does no good to argue that love cannot be forced. A person threatened with loss of love is threatened with loss of self-esteem. The weaker the self-esteem the more desperate the need for love and the more dangerous the jealousy.

The Self and Sex

I have counseled many young women in their middle teens who had become sexually promiscuous. It turned out frequently that father had failed them between ages of three and six. At that time he stood for all men in their lives. He was not home much of the time because he was too busy. When he was there he was too tired to pay much attention to them. He considered this their mother's responsibility anyway. They were not given the assurance that they were acceptable, desirable, worthful, lovable little female persons. Because of his attitude toward them doubts were created in their mind, anxiety was increased and by the time they reached adolescence it all added up to a sizable fear—a fear that they were not lovable.

When they discovered how sex could be used to attract boys, they set out to prove to themselves that they were desirable, worthful, lovable female persons. The trouble was that it did not prove what they wanted it to prove. It increased their anxiety and desperation because of their mounting guilt and lack of regard for themselves. In the counseling process there was no need to focus on sex. It was only symptomatic anyway. The entire problem rooted in their self-image and self-esteem. As this was gradually strengthened through the counseling process, their behavior changed of its own accord.

This kind of anxiety about the adequacy or acceptability of the self as an emerging man is behind much sexual promiscuity on the part of boys. Though multiple causation operates with respect to sex behavior there is little doubt that a great deal of it is for the simple purpose of trying to prove manliness to the self. This is partly accomplished by proving it to others on the part of those still dependent on others for how they think and feel about themselves. Hence, there is considerable bragging on the part of both boys and girls about sexual conquests which give them status. In this respect they are not much different from the rest of us except in age.

The importance of the self-image and self-regard for successful marriage cannot be overrated. Much conflict between husbands and wives is nothing but a desperate effort to bolster the self-regard. Much unhappiness may be attributed to lack of security, an inaccurate self-image and an inadequate self-regard. The compulsive need on the part of so many men to be the head of the house, dominate the entire family, and achieve the kind of success that will enable them to drive two cars and build in suburbia is a confession of inferiority feeling, inaccurate self-image, and inadequate self-regard.

Inferiority feelings in adulthood are said to be the mainspring for extreme competitiveness. It is the drive behind the kind of success that carries with it ulcers and heart trouble. It is the compulsion behind much cigarette smoking and drinking. Some of this behavior is intended to say, "See what a big man or woman I am—really sophisticated!" Such behavior is not confined to youth. Adults who have the same desperate need to be accepted act the same way.

Much of modern advertising appeals to people who do not have much respect and regard for themselves. The psychologists employed by the advertisers well know that many people depend upon what they have by way of possessions to establish this image of themselves and this regard for themselves. Most of the advertisements say in effect, "With this thing you can be somebody." This dependence upon the impression made on others with whatever status symbol is an indication that we cannot depend on our self. The self has remained weak and childish. Our efforts to compensate are proof of our immaturity.

In dealing with our children from the earliest days of their lives we are both supporting and threatening their developing concepts of themselves and feelings about themselves. It is extremely important that we supply sufficient love to be reassuring, sufficient recognition and praise for their achievements to give them confidence. We must believe in them enough for them to come to believe in themselves. We must trust them enough to help them trust themselves. We must reveal sufficient acceptance so that they may come to accept themselves. It will influence all their relationships, especially those in marriage. It will determine to great measure whether they can be competent parents.

Here is a married man who is dating a girl half his age. Either she is flattered by his attention or she is a deliberate gold digger. In either case her attitude toward him supplies him with feelings about himself that his wife cannot or will not supply. Perhaps he cannot admire himself unless he thinks of himself as young. She helps him to feel young. Perhaps his wife has resisted or rejected him sexually. This is a direct attack upon his masculinity and it can produce impotency. The girl gives him back his sense of adequacy—in short, his potency. Basically she inflates his self-esteem. Husbands and wives pay a tremendous price for failure to support each other at the heart of life, the self-concept and self-regard.

In their struggle to grow up, children and young people are forever revealing their needs. They are forever striving to secure satisfaction and fulfillment of those needs. In the next chapter we shall make an effort to understand their preoccupation with getting.

5

Satisfying
Their
Needs
to
Get

W HAT DOES "satisfying children's needs to get" have to
do with preparing them for marriage? Unless they are
helped to satisfy their needs they may go into marriage with
childhood needs still unmet. In that case, in trying to satisfy
such needs they may wreck their marriage. Many a marriage
is threatened by the compulsive clamor, the dangerous demands, the inevitable exploitation of a marriage partner by a
spouse who is desperately trying to satisfy unfulfilled childhood needs. The woman who goes through a string of marriages and divorces may be hopelessly in search of a father in
each new husband. The man who wants to go and come as
he pleases, to spend his free time with "the boys" and who
explodes if his wife complains has probably missed among
other things, appropriate mothering. What then do children
need that has significance for their marriages later?

The infant's greatest need is for *security*. The need is in
direct ratio to its helplessness. There is little surprise, there-

fore, at the infant's preoccupation with its mother. All is well as long as she is there and available. If she is not there and cannot be produced, fear may create hysteria in the infant. Because of its insecurity and the mother's relation to its security the infant must possess its mother completely. If anyone comes along who appears to the infant to be threatening, who might take the mother away, the infant is immediately frightened and angry. It can be extreme because fear can be extreme. It was a wise providence that gave an infant a very small body. The same fears and anger in a person with an adult body in marriage produce tragic behavior that we read about in the newspapers. Always damaging, many times fatal, it is all tied up with the infant's need to get security and to possess the source of it.

We Help Them to Get

As the infant emerges into childhood and begins to do things for itself, it is getting ability to extend its movements, to explore beyond a crib. It needs attention and gets that increasingly by either being good or being bad. If we study the needs of children we shall understand a great deal of their behavior, which is mainly efforts to secure fulfillment of those needs. Too many adults show an infantile need to get. They never did receive satisfyingly. They are now compulsively driven to get. They do not make good marriage partners.

Among the newer needs confronting all children in our country today are the needs to become acquainted with and to learn to use a vast array of new mechanical devices. Either we provide opportunity for them to meet this need or we interfere and force them to learn somewhere else. Children must also learn how to meet friends and strangers and deal with others in general. They are confronted with compari-

son and competition, with success and failure, with changing
standards of values. They will be confronted with attitudes
of friendliness or unfriendliness, love and hate, and many
strange ways of thinking, feeling, and doing things in our
modern mixed-up world.

In our dealing with them, if we support them and give
them confidence, they become increasingly adept in dealing
with this world. If we threaten them we create fears, raise
doubts, and make them inept in dealing with their surround-
ings. We need to remember that children are impressed by
whatever impresses us. Our influence goes far beyond any
moment when we are attempting to tell or teach them directly. They are forever getting from us even when we are
not aware that we are giving. They get ideas and feelings
about the world in general, about us, and about themselves
in particular.

Have you noticed that the outside world seems to be a
reflection of the inner condition? If the child, young person
or adult feels all right within himself, then the world is all
right. If he feels unsure, insecure, unable to regard himself
or trust himself then the world is an insecure place, people
are not trustworthy, and there are many anxieties and fears
about it.

Selfishness Is Misunderstood

One of the most misleading ideas about children is that
they are selfish. If they are, it is because the Creator made
them that way. As already asserted, children, because they
need, must be preoccupied with getting and with themselves in the getting process. It is necessary to their growth
and development. Selfishness is a term that ought to be
restricted for use among adults. Any adult who should have
gotten but has not and must therefore continue to strive to

get, perhaps with disregard of, or at the expense of others, might legitimately be considered selfish. Even in such a case, the selfishness should be understandable and ought not to be condemned as we do frequently in our self-rightousness. Only the self that has gotten adequately across the years according to its needs is in a position to be unselfish. Before we can give we must get.

This functions not only with respect to material things but with regard to those characteristics of personality which are most influential in our success or failure in marriage. Before an adult can trust he has to become trustworthy. He has to get a kind of dependability and integrity that will enable him to trust himself. It is a common observation that we tend to suspect in others what we are guilty of ourselves. There are too many husbands and wives who cannot really trust each other. Many times it is because they cannot trust themselves. Perhaps they were not trusted enough as children.

I once knew a so-called "congenital liar." This person had been so unsure and insecure that he tried to defend himself through misrepresentations. One lie required another. They seemed to be sufficiently effective, and so he fell into the habit. It became his way of dealing with life. He came to me because he had met a young woman in whom he wanted to believe. He was very much concerned because he was unable to believe her. She could have been as trustworthy as a saint and as strong as the Rock of Gibraltar, but he still would not have been able to believe her. The problem did not lie in her, but in him. He did not have enough trust-worthiness within himself to be able to believe.

A certain woman came to me expressing her fears and anxieties because of a disintegrating marriage. It became apparent that she was a perfectionist. It showed up every-where, but most noticeably in her housekeeping. It was clear that she was a very poor companion to her husband. This is very frequently the case. Here was a woman who desperately needed to be loved and was not sure that she was worthy of it. Because she could not feel sure that she was worthy of it, she could not accept it when it was offered. In compensation she tried to prove her worthfulness by her performance as a housekeeper. As a result of her own inner frustration and conflict she developed attitudes toward her husband that were driving him away. She had never gotten and was not in a position to give, nor could she gracefully receive.

Have you noticed that those who seem to be able to give attention have already secured adequate attention? ... those who seem to be able to give compliments have already received compliments in great abundance? ... those who are able to praise have themselves received praise to a great extent? ... those who can love have been abundantly loved? These are the healthy ones.

The giving must be genuine. It must be a gift. When we pay compliments to secure compliments or win approval it is bribery, not a gift. When we give attention in order to get anything, we bribe. When we praise to make people like us instead of to make them feel good we are getting, not giving. If we have not gotten adequately in these and other ways we are more likely to use our giving as bribery. There is a direct relationship between the getting in early life and the giving in later life.

Self-Satisfaction Is Derived Through Giving

There comes a time when, if we have grown up, if we have received adequately across the years, we no longer seem to derive the same kind of happiness or the same amount of satisfaction from continuing our efforts to get. We may make the wonderful discovery that there is a new kind of happiness and satisfaction that comes through giving. At Christmas time, during childhood, preoccupied with getting things we may still give joyously because of the approval we get from the giving. It is approval that comes from others—parents, relatives, and friends. The basic need is approval. The giving is only a means to that end. If we do not get adequately across the years then we go into adulthood still giving for the purpose of getting approval.

This is not true giving in an adult. By the time we reach adulthood the approval should have been transferred from outside ourselves to within ourselves. We should give because we approve of ourselves giving. We are not dependent upon approval from anyone else at the time. We give whether there is any expression of approval or even thanks from the recipient. Our joy is in the giving alone. This is the kind of capacity that makes for the best marriage. It is required for the most competent parenthood. If we can express our love through the giving of ourselves to the loved one we benefit not only from the results in their life and the resultant attitude they make take toward us, *but mostly from the way we think and feel about ourselves because we give.*

A movie was made in England portraying the development of the jet airplane. Efforts to break the sound barrier failed. Everyone was trying to understand why. The test pilot came up with the crazy idea that instead of pulling the controls toward him in trying to pull out of the dive, he might push them forward. According to all the laws of aerodynamics understood up to that time, this was ridiculous. It should throw the airplane into an outside loop and rip off the wings.

One airplane crashed. When the new airplane was built and the second test pilot took it up, he determined to try out the theory. When he had finished all the required checks and they ordered him down he refused, saying that he was going to test his idea. They went into hysterics on the ground, and he broke off communication with them. When he had climbed to the approximate ceiling for the airplane and kicked it over into a power dive and approached the speed of sound the controls froze just as they had before. The plane began to buffet as if it would come apart. The pilot took a deep breath and shoved the controls forward. He came out of the power dive and went through the sound barrier with a sonic boom.

It was not known until that time that in order to break the sound barrier the controls have to be reversed. How like life that principle is. In order to break the childhood barrier, the controls have to be reversed. Until we become mature adults we must be preoccupied with getting. Everything must come toward us. It is only when we reach the point where we can derive greater satisfaction from extending ourself toward others in a giving way that we can break through the childhood barrier and become mature adults. One does not need much imagination to understand how significant this can be in marriage.

Giving Is Essential to Parenthood

Far too many children are born to parents who must continue to get when they ought to be at a stage where they could give in response to the needs of their child. Instead, they will exploit the child in efforts to satisfy their own needs. Many a mother is so anxious and unsure of herself, of her own acceptability, desirability, and worthfulness in the social whirl that she will shape her little girl, through dancing lessons and otherwise, to perform in ways that will enable her vicariously to have the experience herself. Many children are exploited by parents attempting to live their lives through their children. They cannot give of themselves in response to the child's needs. They must use the child in the fulfillment of their own needs.

Since many of us who are parents have not yet accepted ourselves we tend to reject in our children whatever it is that we have not accepted in ourselves. We are likely to discipline most violently when we see in our children what we do not like in ourselves. We must acquire a better understanding of ourselves as human beings. We must be able to accept ourselves with our strengths and weaknesses if we are to be good parents to our children. We must learn to like ourselves, must indeed love ourselves if we are to be the best parents for our children.

A Capacity to Give Is a Qualification for Marriage

Many a battle rages in marriage because both the husband and the wife need, and neither is capable of giving according to the needs of the other. They will be demanding and exploitative and angry because of refusal or rejection. When a wife needs reassurance and a husband can supply it, fulfillment and satisfaction come to both. When a husband needs encouragement and a wife can supply it, he has strength with which to face an unpredictable and foreboding future. When one needs confidence and the other extends it through belief that the needful one can accomplish whatever it is in his own way, this kind of respect is the most valuable nourishment for confidence.

It is well understood among psychologists, as previously stated, that most of what we criticize and complain about in others and the world outside ourselves is a revelation of what we do not like in ourselves. It reflects areas where we have not gotten adequately and must now, on the adult level, continue to strive to get. This compulsive striving does produce some of our best business executives and leaders in religion and politics. It gives us some of our most famous movie kings and queens. But the apparent success is in many cases a front behind which frequently hides a frightened, sometimes terrified, dwarf who was made a dwarf by inadequate getting during the years of childhood and youth.

Here is a woman who has secured prominence as a very competent social and cultural leader, but she cannot give warm affectionate companionship to her own daughter. Here is a man who has all the symbols of success in terms of business position, home, automobiles, and friends, but he cannot give affectionate companionship to his own wife. Here is a woman who is on the board of Mental Health and concerned about delinquency, but she cannot manage her relationships with her own son. Here is a man who has become famous for his philanthropic enterprises and his love for humanity, but he has a son who was kicked out of school and jumped into an unwise marriage to avoid a forced marriage with another girl.

It is noticeable that parents who cannot give themselves, frequently give things. They feel guilty in a vague sort of way and want to salve their conscience by doing penance. "Things" are the compensatory penance. They are a poor substitute for warm, close, affectionate parenthood. But parents who never had that kind of parenthood may not be able to be that kind of parent, at least without counseling help. Much of life's misery seems to be the result of mistaken attempts to get happiness. It also reflects inadequate getting through childhood and youth. Happy are those parents and children who know the richness and abundance of life where the getting and the giving are fairly well balanced.

In the next chapter we shall consider one of the most important needs in any human being. We shall examine what happens if this need is not fulfilled. We shall see again the relation between the getting and the giving in the most important experiences in human relationships.

6

*Fostering
Their
Feelings
of
Affection*

THERE is a religious saying that we love because God first loved us. However that may be, it is well established that we love as men and women according to whether we were loved by our parents when we were infants. We love as our exposure to love has stimulated our response and developed our capacity. In loving, a husband or a wife reflects all his or her loving experience.

Infantile Love Is Self-Love

The infant's first experience with love is through the mother's concern for it. She pets it and cuddles it. She nurses it and bathes it. She removes its discomfort. She brings it all kinds of pleasures. She pays attention to it. She concentrates upon it. The infant feels highly valued because of all this. Quite an impression is made and the impression is that it is of great worth. If she loves herself loving her baby the infant feels this too. Unless she can revel in self-love as she loves her baby the rest may be mechanical and miss the infant's greatest need. Its first reaction to being loved, therefore, is self-love. It begins to think and feel about itself the way the mother does. As it continues to grow and other people show their love for it, this first impression is supported. The attitudes of others add to its own self-love.

When the infant becomes a child he continues to value himself by the way he is valued. If he is praised, he feels worthy. If he is blamed and criticized, he feels unworthy. If attention is paid, he is a person of importance. If no attention is paid to him and he is neglected, he is thrown back upon himself to try to prove his own importance. This he may do by becoming a clinging vine or by achieving in enterprises that bring him admiration and esteem. He must strive to establish self-love.

Overindulgence on the part of a parent can mislead a child into thinking that it is worth overly much and that he ought to have that kind of expression of his worth from everyone else. The child is unsatisfied with smaller amounts of attention. As he grows he must struggle to secure the amount originally offered by the parent and he becomes greedy and highly demanding in his hunger for love. Such a person, as an adult, finds it very difficult to feel safe and secure with strangers. Such a person cannot bear to be alone.

There was, for instance, a woman who was a very attractive person. She was animated and alive when she was with friends. She appeared very much at ease and seemed to enjoy herself with relaxed pleasure until a stranger appeared and was introduced. Immediately she put on a "poker face" and withdrew into a quiet aloofness. Her friends noticed it and tried to bring her out of it. Not until the stranger left would she let down her guard and reveal herself as her friends knew her.

We all have minor tendencies in this direction under similar circumstances. The strange always brings a feeling of uneasiness. We usually get over it in a little while. It is only when we cannot get over it that it becomes a matter of concern. In the instance of the woman mentioned, it was possible to trace the origin to parental treatment during her childhood.

On the other hand, if a child has been inadequately loved, he may conclude that he is unworthy of love. Such a person as an adult may find it very difficult to accept love from others. He remains remote and stand-offish and cannot respond easily to love when it is offered. There seems to be a direct connection between one's capacity to love and one's having been loved in infancy and early childhood. Many a husband and wife reflect it.

Jealousy Is Inevitable

Since the infant's security in the universe is all tied up with its complete possession of its mother, father emerges as its first great threat. How the infant is helped to accept the father into its love relationship and its feeling of security may influence the way it deals with the outside world for the rest of its life. We have all heard a little child cry fretfully or anxiously when the father returns and takes mother into his arms. The child may tug on its mother's dress and attempt to push the father away. If the child is picked up by the mother and included in the embrace, it may still want to shove the father away until it is sufficiently reassured that there is no real danger in this presence of the father within the mother's concern.

About the time the infant is sufficiently reassured with regard to father, a brother or sister may come on the scene. This is a new invader and it competes immediately for the attention and concern formerly possessed exclusively by the first child. Some parents are fairly good in helping the first child to anticipate the arrival of a second; but, in any event, the first child will need an unusual amount of attention and show of concern, perhaps an overindulgence of affectionate regard for a little while, just to reassure it that this second child is not going to take its mother completely away from him.

As previously stated, jealousy is fundamentally fear of losing possession and anger directed toward any real or supposed threat. It originates in a sense of inadequacy or helplessness and it is characteristic of infancy and early childhood. It will crop up again in early adolescence at which time the young person is thrown into a situation with the outside world and his age mates, where he is keenly aware of his own inadequacies and incompetencies. He needs the security of complete possession of some loving one.

If additional brothers and sisters come along across the years, the older children begin to understand that the arrival of young ones will not necessarily threaten too much or destroy their security. If we could only realize that the one thing children need above everything else is love and that this is more important than food, clothing, and shelter, we might more universally meet the needs of the young; for love is a commodity which cannot be purchased or coerced. It can only be given. Of course, we can give it only according to our capacity to love ourselves and to give—which in turn is the result of our experiences with love and how it was given to us in our youngest years.

Ambivalence Is Characteristic of Children

Because we are secure and insecure at the same time as children we can easily develop the capacity to love and hate at the same time. Ambivalence is characteristic of all children. No normal child ever grows up without both loving and hating his parents and his brothers and sisters. We have seen what hate can do at its worst and have condemned it. We have gone to such an extreme in condemning that we have made it necessary for many people to deny that they ever did or ever do hate. It seems unthinkable to them that they could possibly feel this way about someone from whom they have received much across the years and toward whom there should be a show of respect, loyalty, and love.

Many a young person has clearly indicated hate of a father or a mother in manner and tone of voice only to deny it vehemently when his counselor suggested it. Many a husband or wife has revealed hate for a mate only to react with shock and denial when the counselor called it to his or her attention.

One reason that children learn to love *and* hate parents is that there are no perfect parents. That means that there will be some times when parents are unlovable or actually hateful. The normal response of a healthy child to a hateful parent is hate. But they love and they hate us because also we love and we hate them. Such a statement would throw some parents into panic because of a lack of understanding about how life actually develops across the years. Again, our guilt and our desire to be respectable and good may cause us to deny that we ever hate our own children. We make an effort to soften it up by changing the word to something like "dislike." This does not contain quite so much danger as the word hate.

How any given parent expresses love will have great influence on the development of the appetite and expectation of love on the part of the children. Later a husband or wife may feel loved according to whether the same expression is forthcoming from their mate. They tend to express their love for their mate along the lines of their childhood experience. Since husbands and wives come from different family backgrounds and with parentage of different capacities to love and different ways of expressing it, there can be considerable difference in any marriage. People sometimes feel very much unloved because the husband or wife is not expressing love in the way in which it was expected—that is, in the way in which this person had been taught from infancy to expect it.

Perhaps more significantly for marriage our image of ourself and our feelings about ourself depend to great measure upon how we were loved by the parent of the opposite sex. There are many teen-agers who flounder around amidst sexual promiscuities and other forms of delinquency because they have not been helped to feel sure about themselves. Prostitution and homosexuality, in many instances, can be traced back to parental negligence or rejection. Some roots of misery, vice, and crime run back to inadequate loving on the part of parents.

When our children compete as they do across the growing-up years—not only in achievement and social behavior, but for our approval and for our love—there is always considerable bickering and rivalry that may express itself in open conflict. As our children begin to find friends outside the family and to secure expressions of love from them, the conflict within the family tends to diminish. You may have noticed how, when children begin to go to school, to get away from the family, and to establish friendships or fall in love in the early teens, they begin to show love for each other within the family far more than ever before. This is most noticeable in the middle and late teens as they approach adulthood.

Romantic Love Dawns in the Teens

Most early loves in the teens are highly romantic. That is to say, they are full of fantasy. The other person, for the time being, seems to possess all the attributes of the ideal. Such love we refer to as infatuation. It is not difficult to identify because it usually flares into being swiftly. It causes a couple to feel that nothing else matters. There is one overwhelming desire and that is to be together. The emotional pressure is in the direction of expressing their love for each other through physical contact. Kissing, holding hands, embracing, fondling—all these acts lead to struggle against engaging in premarital sex relations as the most intimate expression of their love for each other. They are thrown into controversy because of religious belief or social moralities. They may have considerable struggle within themselves and between themselves, or they may succumb to their desires at some risk and with an increasing load of guilt.

Many times infatuation causes a couple to rationalize whatever it is they want to do because they are in love. The romantic illusions about love with which our country is well saturated support this trend. They make romantic love the highest value and use it to justify almost anything. It is not surprising therefore that a couple could feel that such love would solve all their problems, that it would make up for any lacks or shortcomings in each other, or in their relationship.

One of the most characteristic signs of infatuation is the feeling that it will last forever. Nothing lasts forever, and love changes as people change across the years. Many persons have concluded that they no longer love each other because they do not love as they once did. This is as silly as saying, I am no longer myself because I do not look as I once did. It limits love to only one kind of expression and experience at one time in life. We may love many times. We could love the same person many ways across a period of time.

Because of the power of infatuation, and because as parents we remember with some anxiety the experiences when we were in love during the teens, we tend to become frightened when such a love affair develops in the life of one of our children. We know something of its power and its capacity to distort values and supersede judgment. Some of us have not gotten beyond this stage in our own growth and have had several love affairs of this type since marriage. This tends to make us even more anxious and fearful of such experiences in the loves of our young people.

It may be observed that love is personality expression. If kindness is characteristic of a person, kindness will be in his or her loving. If a person is unkind, unkindness will creep into his loving. If the person is confident, his loving will show it. If he is anxious, anxiety will crop up in the love relationship. The person who is dependable will be able to trust and manifest it in loving. The person who is full of deceit will not be able to trust and will be made miserable by suspicion. A person who is basically selfish, who must continue to strive to get, will be incapable of being generous even to the loved one. His love will be a demand or a bribe, an exploitation rather than an enriching and fulfilling, giving expression.

We hear a great deal about love at first sight. Such love is quite possible, but it is not the sort of love with which it is advisable to approach marriage. A love that is mature enough for marriage may have some of the elements of romantic love in it, but it is basically a genuine fondness quite apart from any advantage to be gained for the self. It develops only through continued experience together across a period of time. There will likely be some need for reassurance because of the recognition of personal imperfection, but this need for reassurance is not distorted and abnormal to the point of anxiety.

More Mature Love Has a "We" Outlook

There is a tendency on the part of a person with a capacity for love which is mature enough for marriage to be concerned about the well-being of the loved one. This concern may be as great as for himself. The religious suggestion that we ought to love our neighbor as we love ourself rests upon the psychological consideration that we have grown up in such manner as to love ourselves well. Mature love tends to consider the loved person as a better person. That is partly what makes him or her so desirable. When two persons commit themselves to each other, they do in fact become a part of each other. They exchange the "I" orientation in life for a "we" outlook and feel considerable happiness in this union.

In early adolescence one loves because of anxiety and doubt, because of feelings of inferiority and a very great need for reassurance. When one has become strong within himself he is confident and feels secure. He can give of himself generously even to the point of sacrifice. Such giving usually is, but does not have to be, counterbalanced with a return from the loved one. The satisfaction derived through the giving is sufficient to the loving one. Early love is possessive; a more mature love recognizes the individuality and the independence of the loved one.

If we in dealing with our children and young people across the years can help them to understand through our own experience with them and through what we say to them that love is different for different ages and stages along the way through life and that it changes as we change, there is less likelihood of disillusion and despair in their marriage later on. Of everything that we do for them, what we do to help them learn to love is probably the most important contribution we make. Love is the most important factor in all life. It is the greatest civilizing power and the only power that may ultimately do away with war—both war in the home and in the family of man on the planet Earth.

Though we cannot claim total responsibility for the way in which our children grow into young people and adults, we nevertheless are still powerfully influential in their development. The way we express our love for them from infancy all the way across the years will determine to a great extent the way they will be able to love their own wives or husbands and children.

Love and sex are related but not synonymous. Sex attracts and frightens us. We have experienced ecstasy and misery, satisfaction and anxiety because of it. When our children reach puberty and begin to show signs of a new awareness of sexual attraction we begin to worry. In the next chapter we shall examine ways through which we may be of help to our children and young people as they struggle to understand and manage the sex forces in their lives.

7

Guiding Them Through Their Sexual Experiences

THE OTHER DAY a parent of a ten-year-old boy asked me for a book on sex. The parent said that he wanted to make sure that his son got a good sex education. Before recommending a book I talked with this parent about the sex education his son already had. It is never a question of whether we should give our children an education with regard to sex. We have been doing that from the moment they were born. The question is—what kind?

Sex Life Begins in Infancy

The way in which the mother responds to the infant's exploration of his own body and the accidental or deliberate touching of his own genitals, the manner in which the mother nurses her baby or bottle-feeds it, and her behavior revealing her feelings about him—these are the earliest influences in the life of anyone with respect to sex. Education is already in process. Those mothers who feel that sex is low and debasing, dirty or wrong, those who are embarrassed and self-conscious at any reference to sex will pass their feelings on to their children in spite of themselves. Children feel us long before they can understand us. Those mothers who recognize sex as a part of God's creation, as clean and healthy unless made otherwise, those mothers who are casual and relaxed, who enjoy their own sexual expression of affection with their husbands will pass on their feelings to their children.

Toilet training is the next area in which the young life is conditioned as far as sex is concerned. Here attitudes and feelings of the mother are conditioning factors in the child's feelings about itself too. Here may emerge the first great struggle between child and parent. It is a struggle for power and dominance. The toilet becomes the battleground. The experience becomes more than the controlled elimination of waste materials from the body. It becomes a personality struggle. The genitals are involved and included in the conditioning process. Parents who can make this as natural and casual a learning experience with least conflict contribute most to their children's healthy sex life.

The third area of experience within which sex education takes place is childhood questions and childhood play. The big risk in this area is parental reading into childhood words and behavior adult interpretations, and responding accordingly. A mother catching her small daughters examining each other's genitals at bedtime is shocked and frightened by adult images of lesbianism, and explodes at her children with supercharged emotional concern. She has no idea of the possible emotional damage she may have done. Another mother coming upon a similar situation might respond to childish curiosity with permissive understanding. Her relaxed manner in helping them into night clothes and tucking them in bed might allow them the satisfaction of curiosity and the escape from any frightening experience that would etch itself into unconscious memory.

We are not all free from the constricted inhibitions of puritanical prudery. Sex is not dealt with nor discussed naturally in all homes to this day. In many homes any mention is likely to be met with punishment. Punishment can range from a verbal reprimand by the parents to isolation from the family, by the child's being sent to his room, or actual physical punishment in the form of spanking. The ignorant practice of washing out a child's mouth with soapsuds because it had spoken a word referring to sex has not altogether passed from the scene. It is no wonder that children get the impression that sex is a dirty word.

Parental Policy Is Important

If parents use the policy of punishment, they give the impression that sex is rejectable. Because of their indefiniteness about it, sex can take on the attributes of all the fearfulness of the unknown. Curiosity is inflated sometimes to a morbid degree. Here are roots of much of man's preoccupation with the female body, expressed in the behavior of peeping Toms, and the wide sales of pornographic literature. Here are roots for much guilt from one's own groping, blundering explorations with respect to sex. A policy of punishment forces a child outside the home for whatever information or misinformation it may be able to pick up in out-of-the-way places. The emotional attitudes characteristic of toilet conversations or secret whisperings in hidden corners are certainly not conducive to the best experience of sex in life.

Other parents may proceed with a policy of evasion. When questions are asked they will postpone or pass the buck to the church, or the school, or a doctor, or to the same-sex parent as the child. The immediate consequence is not so likely to be traumatic, although curiosity is further aroused. Why can't the answer be given straightforwardly as with any other question? The simple answer to a three-year-old's question about where babies come from is that they grow inside their mothers. For most children of that age such an answer is sufficient. Older children may ask how the baby gets out. Again, a simple statement that it is growing in a sack that is upside down and with the opening kept closed until time for the baby to be born, may be satisfying. If not, it may be further stated that there is an opening provided especially for the baby to come out at the right time. It is important that mother's answers be simple and honest, but the emotional attitude of the mother in answering is even more important in the education of the child. The end result of evasion, if that is used, is the same as with punishment. The child is forced outside the home for whatever it is trying to find out about sex. Much sex play among children is stimulated by curiosity and has little more meaning. But adults can panic about it and give it frightening meaning.

Some parents in their anxiety to keep sex pure and holy overdo it, making it so sacred as to be untouchable, undiscussable, and altogether out of this world. Any experience with sex therefore becomes a smear on the page of life or somehow a violation of God's will.

Wise parents will accept the infant's preoccupation with his body and exploration of it as it endeavors to find out about itself and the rest of the universe close at hand. Toilet training may be accomplished without too much anxiety and punishment, and accepted as a natural function of life. Young children may be allowed to observe each other and their parents without any clothes and satisfy their natural curiosity with respect to male and female anatomy within the casual accepting love-supported security of the family.

When sex questions come from children, wise parents will deal with them as normal and legitimate questions. Where babies come from may be discussed with a daughter approaching puberty or a son about the same time with an explanation of the significance of menstruation, the fertilization of the female ovum by the male sperm, and a general outline of pregnancy. Such parents understand that questions will continue to come across the years, because at no time will any answer satisfy the curiosity of any child with respect to everything in its experience.

Information can be imparted as needed. One of the best helps for parents of young children is *Facts of Life for Children* by Adie Suehsdorf.* It is important that such facts be imparted in an emotional atmosphere that makes them normal and acceptable within the experience of the child. The sad fact is that many parents cannot respond normally and naturally to their children's questions about sex. Their own mixed emotions or disturbing experiences interfere. Such parents will find books for their children and young people useful supplemental instruments.

Living conditions may make it difficult for parents to satisfy their own sex needs without exposing their children to sexual intercourse at an early age. Some children are witness to sexual infidelity or they become aware of it on the part of one or both parents. Some are molested by neurotic adults while they are still children. Parents would do well to consult a child psychologist or some other specialist who might determine if such an experience was traumatic. In that event the child would need help to reduce the threat of the experience to the rest of its life, especially to its marriage later. Children all have the problem of dealing with incestuous

---

* Documentation for books mentioned in the text will be found under the author's name in the bibliography at the end of this book.

feelings within the family. The development of understanding and the control of desire is not easy in our culture. Our children need our help, and many of us could benefit from the help of child psychologists in our efforts in behalf of our children. If we cannot talk with one, at least we may read what they have to say.

As children enter school and learn to read, books which deal with sex in life may be secured and made a part of the family library. Doctors, ministers, and counselors at school are good sources for reference to such books. Children from such homes are less likely to be abnormally curious and much more sure of themselves as they approach the years of adolescence, and sex becomes more active in their social relationships.

Among some good books for young children, up to twelve or thereabouts are *The Wonderful Story of How You Were Born*, by Sidonie Gruenberg; and *Being Born*, by Frances Bruce Strain.

For children twelve and over, Roy Dickerson's *So Youth May Know* is still widely used. In addition you might secure Ruth Fedder's *A Girl Grows Up*. Dr. B. S. Gottlieb's two books *What a Boy Should Know About Sex* and *What a Girl Should Know About Sex* have been used by many parents. Lois Pemberton's *The Stork Didn't Bring You* is well liked by junior high age children.

Some parents discover that their son or daughter is masturbating. Parental reaction to such erotic stimulation can make quite a difference to a boy or girl. Present estimates suggest that about 95 per cent of all men and boys at one time have or presently do seek this form of sexual satisfaction. About 70 per cent of all girls and women are estimated to engage in self-stimulation. Modern medicine including psychiatry states flatly that there is no ground for all the dire consequences once believed to follow masturbation.

Inflated guilt feelings, however, may seriously threaten unless relieved. The only other real threat is the arresting of psychosexual development at such an infantile level that masturbation is preferred to normal sexual intercourse in marriage. There is no reason why it should not continue into marriage unless it is a competitive substitute for coitus. Mutual masturbation may become a part of foreplay or an occasional means of satisfaction within marriage if the couple so desire. If we understand this, our attitude will be more emotionally balanced when any situation develops which might make it necessary for us to discuss it with our young sons or daughters.

The Taboos Are Broken

The old conspiracy of silence has been partially destroyed. During the first half of the twentieth century particularly, we have begun to discover a great deal more about the part sex plays in life. When we broke free from the prison of Victorian puritanical prudery, we began to acquire more enlightenment with respect to sex. At the same time we created a situation in which it was possible for us to move past freedom into license. It is interesting to read that the ancient civilizations outlawed romantic love because they felt that it increased sex license to such a degree that the civilization itself was threatened. Apparently sex, like any other impulse capable of wonderful enrichment and fulfillment in life, is also capable of much violation and destructiveness and must be understood and controlled. The degree to which we have accomplished this in our own lives marks the degree to which we are able to be of most use to our children as they grow into manhood and womanhood and approach marriage.

When dating begins, or along in high school when going

steady becomes the pattern, father-son and mother-daughter conversations may cover parking and petting and questions of premarital sexual intercourse. Among matters discussed might be the findings of Lester Kirkendall showing that boys and men are most likely to have sex relations with pick-ups, girls in whom they have no interest and about whom they are not concerned. They are less likely to cohabit with acquaintances, still less with friends and least likely with the girl with whom they are in love. Boys and men tend to become protective about that which they value highest.

Girls on the other hand are not prone to have sexual intercourse with strangers. Some are willing to cohabit with acquaintances. They are more likely to do so with friends and most likely to submit to, if not actually seek, coitus with the boy or man with whom they are in love. This radical difference between boys and girls and men and women is a cause of much confusion and misunderstanding.

These differences can be short-circuited by anxiety or fear, by a compulsive need for reassurance or to prove masculinity or sensual femininity, in defiance or revenge. But these differences are, unless interfered with by unconscious motivations, characteristic of the sexes in general. Implications of these differences or other motivations may be a part of parental discussions with their young.

With groups of young people I have a way of talking about petting which they seem to appreciate. I have used the same procedure with individuals including my own daughters and son. It rests upon the assumption that premarital sexual intercourse is unwise and that a person or couple do not want to "go all the way," as the young people put it. They are entitled to our reasons for such an assumption or at least to face the question, "Why not go all the way?" We shall come to that, but for the moment we are concerned with the matter of petting. As I use the term, "petting" is any part or all of the arousal process whereby anyone causes anyone else to become sexually excited, and excites himself at the same time. It goes all the way from the first physical contacts up to and including sexual intercourse. The following diagram has been helpful:

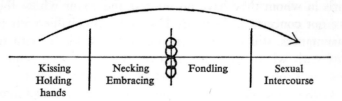

| | Kissing
Holding
hands | Necking
Embracing | Fondling | Sexual
Intercourse |

The division of the diagram into four sections is arbitrary, and their equal size is deceptive. What matters is that we can see the progress from left to right, from first physical contacts to more ardent and more intimate contact. Fondling means the touching or rubbing of the more sexually excitable parts of the body; in the female, the breast, and in both, the genitals. Sexual intercourse is self-evident. The long curving arrow left to right is representative of the fact that any progress through the various stages of the diagram is petting. The process of arousal, of stimulating sexual excitement, is the petting process.

If a couple do not want to go all the way into sexual intercourse they must stop somewhere short of it. Where should they stop? Parents will answer that question differently. I suggest that they stop between the necking and the fondling, where the spiral line divides the diagram in half. The reason is simple. Up to that point most young people have themselves under control. Beyond that point a girl may have a physical fight on her hands if she is determined not to permit sexual intercourse. If a couple love and respect each other the chances are that they will come to some mutual understanding. If they are going steady the problem is to stick with their mutual agreement. The longer they go steady the more intimate they want to, and are likely to, become. Early dating and going steady can put sexual pressures on a boy and girl beyond their capacity to manage. This is why, even when a young couple is ready for marriage, they may find it hard to refrain from sexual intercourse during their engagement, unless the engagement is entered with a wedding date in sight and not too far away.

Young people differ in their sexual excitability as do the rest of us. Some boys or girls may have to "draw the line" earlier in the petting process. Some may be able to go on into the more intense and intimate experiences of fondling without losing control. But one does not keep on leaning over the edge of a cliff just to see how far before he may lose his balance and fall. Caution is on the side of safety. This analogy is not too good because with sex it is as if somebody were pushing one over the cliff. Aroused sex desire can be quite a push.

We may help our young people to understand themselves better and manage their lives with more confidence if we can listen to what they say and express ourselves in some other manner than to give the impression that we think we are "God Almighty." Both boys and girls have responded appreciatively to the chance to understand the problem of petting from such a discussion. We owe it to them further to let them know that the male is geared differently from the female in regard to the time involved in becoming excited. Males in general are very quickly aroused, almost three times as fast as the female. Girls particularly need to know this. It has to do with whose responsibility it is to draw the line.

Boys tend to be aggressive by nature and especially so with sex. Some are just testing to see how far a girl will let them go. Some are predators for reasons that they themselves do not understand. With all the change toward "equality of the sexes" no *equality of responsibility* in this matter has emerged as a universal guide. My candid advice to parents and girls is that it is the girl who must draw whatever line is drawn. Knowing that the boy is much more easily and quickly aroused she must draw the line sometime before she senses that he might lose control of himself and not on the basis of how she feels, unless she is a girl who is the exception and very quick to arouse.

The person who has had several experiences with petting before marriage is probably better prepared for marriage than a person who has had none. But the person who pets promiscuously is probably not so good a risk in marriage as the person who has not petted at all. This is a discussable assertion. You might explore the "why" with your son or daughter.

Motivations for petting can be many and complex. Among them are a need for popularity, the feeling that one is accepted, going along with the crowd, the feeling of need to belong or the excitement of sexual arousal and the attraction of the forbidden. Consequences are many and varied: guilt, loss of reputation, cheapening of sex, broken relationships, and the stopping of sexual and emotional development at the petting level. Values may be in a better understanding of oneself and those of the opposite sex, realization that one can manage life without getting too badly hurt, self-confidence, and self-regard. It all depends upon what happens.

Most of our sons and daughters want to know why they should not have sexual intercourse before marriage. They may not have discussed it with us, but they have most likely discussed it with their age mates. The breaking of taboos against talking about sex seems to some of them to be withdrawal of restrictions against indulging in sexual relationships. We can help them to think if *we* can think. The risk is that we feel threatened and fearful and become parental tyrants and overprotective.

Until some sure way is found to prevent it and is used universally there is the danger of pregnancy. There is no quick and easy way out of that. With abortion still banned by our society there is no safe way in that direction. Fear of discovery will haunt a couple trapped with an unintended pregnancy, along with inescapable guilt. Rationalizations do not seem to be permanently satisfying. Venereal disease is on the increase among the premarital ages. Reactions when a couple are approaching marriage, or are in marriage, are unpredictable. Perhaps the greatest ignorance is revealed in the oversimplification of sex as physical. In my mind as a counselor I am convinced that it is, instead, overwhelmingly psychological and emotional.

Various ideas, opinions, points of view, and feelings will be expressed in discussion between parents and their maturing young people. The fact that there is communication is the important thing. If we can treat our young sons and daughters as persons struggling with the same kind of problems we face they may begin to realize it and have some sympathetic understanding of us. It is well worth the try.

Husband and Wife Must Understand Sex

Sexual incompatibility exists in marriage sometimes because either or both the husband and the wife have never come to understand themselves sexually, much less the other. Anatomy is easy to see and understand, but psychological and emotional aspects of maleness and femaleness are not. Because of our self-consciousness and embarrassment, our inhibitions with respect to sex, there is less communication between husbands and wives in this area than within any other in their experience. Yet, if they are to understand each other and be able to contribute to the enrichment of each other's lives, there must be communication here as well as elsewhere.

Many husbands and wives do not have an adequate vocabulary with which to discuss their sexual experiences. Such people, as parents, are not very likely to provide the most adequate sex education for their children. Where parents feel limited in this regard, as previously mentioned, there are books now available for both parents and children, which tell the story of life from the moment of conception all the way through to the birth of the baby and follow the development of maleness and femaleness through childhood into youth, to manhood and womanhood.

Among sources for specific help the following are especially useful for parents:

New Ways in Sex Education, by Dorothy Baruch
Sex Attitudes in the Home, by Ralph Eckert—out of print but can perhaps be found in the public library
Sex Facts and Attitudes, by Marion Lerrigo
How to Tell Your Children About Sex, by Clyde M. Narramore

For young people, Evelyn M. Duvall's books *Love and the Facts of Life* and *Sense and Nonsense About Sex* are among the best.

Out of years of counseling people in trouble in their marriages, as far as those who seem to be having difficulty in their sex life are concerned, I find some lack of knowledge with respect to the so-called facts of life, but more need for information and understanding about what is considered normal. There are questions and a great deal of anxiety about when a person might be considered oversexed or undersexed. There may be a very few people who are oversexed or undersexed, but what this usually means is that a husband desires more sex than his wife. His ego requires him to assume that his desires are right and normal, therefore she is undersexed. A wife does not desire so much sexual experience as her husband. Her ego requires that she assume she is right and normal, therefore her husband is oversexed. These expressions usually mean simply difference. A session or two with a doctor or competent marriage counselor would probably be helpful toward more compatibility.

Some husbands and wives brought up in ignorance or brittle prudery have the feeling that there is only one right moral position for sexual intercourse. There are as many positions as imagination can contrive, and no one is any more right or moral than another. The process referred to as petting before marriage becomes foreplay after the wedding and has only the limitations of whatever would be self-defeating. Any kind of sexual stimulation or satisfaction which does not result in physical damage or violate either person's aesthetic sensitivities or become a substitute for normal intercourse is all right. Sex in marriage is not a jigsaw puzzle of fitting anatomy together. It is an explorative, developmental adventure with husband and wife alternating as guides as desire determines. If we can get these facts across to our young adults who are anticipating marriage we will have done much to prepare them for their sexual experiences in it.

There seems to be a tremendous need on the part of youth to prove their masculinity and femininity and about all that is left to them, in view of the fading frames of reference for "masculine" and "feminine," is maleness and femaleness. Sexual conquest of women has for centuries been considered by man a sign of masculinity. Seduction of men by women has been final proof of the power of femininity. But complications develop. Problems of impotency on the part of man and frigidity on the part of women are not at all uncommon in the offices of psychiatrists and marriage counselors.

Ministers and marriage counselors engaged in premarital counseling generally make a practice of referring the couple with whom they are counseling to some physician who is

familiar with the techniques of the premarital medical examination. They suggest that the doctor to whom they go may
be in the best position for consultation regarding the most
desirable and appropriate plan for the spacing of children.
Questions of all kinds may be asked, and trustworthy answers secured.

Many doctors have manuals dealing with sex in marriage
which they give to a couple who come for the premarital
examination. Most textbooks on preparation for marriage
have a chapter on sex adjustment in marriage. There are
manuals dealing exclusively with these relationships available
in most bookstores or from the publishers. Increasing num-
bers of libraries are beginning to make them available. Many
ministers and all competent marriage counselors will have
them.

Among such texts, the following are valuable:

Being Married, by Evelyn Duvall and Reuben Hill
Marriage for Moderns, by Henry A. Bowman
Marriage, by Robert O. Blood
Education for Marriage, by James A. Peterson

A manual dealing more specifically with sex adjustment in
marriage is *A Marriage Manual,* by Abraham and Hannah M.
Stone.

Two excellent books for women are Marie Robinson's
The Power of Sexual Surrender and Dr. Marion Hilliard's
book, *A Woman Doctor Looks at Love and Life.*

There Are Values and Threats in Sexual Morality

Sexual morality is established and maintained by any society for the preservation of itself and the welfare of the individuals who make it up. Those who do not want to have
their desires restrained or their lusts curbed are always in

rebellion against it. Many people resist the idea of morality because of the fanatics who in their self-rightousness push it to such an extreme that it becomes as great a threat as license. We as parents have a responsibility to help our young people understand both the service and the threat of sexual morality.

One way of approaching this might be to raise the question, What happens to our family or our society if everybody does whatever is being proposed? If the answer is "nothing," then there is no need for the morality. If the answer is threat or destruction, then obviously the morality must be maintained. The only remaining question is, Who should be exempt from it and on what grounds should they have special privilege, if anybody should?

Young people can be helped to understand why the free expression of sex is limited ideally in our society to marriage. They might find it more difficult to understand why so many of their elders do not limit it thus. But they have a right to ask, and we have a responsibility to be honest with them. Some parents become dictators and attempt complete control. They may overprotect or drive their children underground in their efforts to be good parents. Many a young person with overly suspicious parents has decided, "I may as well be a wolf, if I'm going to be shot for a wolf."

In our society we overprotect our girls and underprotect our boys. The attitude in the past has been that parents should protect their daughters and men should protect their women. The implication is that the male is a sexual predator and should be free to act as such, curbed only by other men. We are now moving into a period of history and a kind of social organization in a space age where there may have to be mutual responsibility for whatever security and welfare there may be between the sexes.

In the past, adults chaperoned young people in their social relationships, straight on into marriage. Today chaperonage is all but obsolete, and parents have the task of transferring responsibility from themselves to their own young people at a much earlier age than ever before in our history. Whether we can do this with some confidence and peace of mind depends upon how well we have done the job of sex education with them and how responsible they have become. If we have a religious faith and have helped our children to formulate one of their own we may breathe more easily. But there are no guarantees. Come what may, our children need to feel and know that we are for them and will stand by and help however we can if and as they need us.

A great deal of sex behavior in our generation and the younger generation seems to be based upon the assumption that whatever happens before a wedding has nothing to do with what may happen afterward. Some research has turned up very disturbing correlations between premarital promiscuity and extramarital sexual affairs. Though, as previously stated, there is nothing inevitably damning or dooming about a premarital experience, a great deal of guilt and anxiety exists long afterward in marriage because of it. Many a daughter is overdisciplined and overprotected by her father or mother because of their behavior when they were her age.

Again we may observe as stated previously that sexual behavior is personality expression. The kind of person a woman is, finds expression through her sex life too. Knowledge contributes. Ignorance proves costly. Integrity, adequate for fidelity, enables a person to trust. Guilt or the capacity for infidelity dooms a person to suspicion and fear. Unselfishness manifests itself in the abundance of fulfillment. Selfishness ravishes through exploitation and violence.

In attempting to guide our children and young people through their sexual experiences we must be concerned with their total personality. If sexual behavior is personality expression, then certainly an adequate knowledge of the "facts of life" is not enough. Our attitudes and feelings about sex inevitably influence our children's attitudes and feelings and send them into their marriage well prepared or ill prepared as far as we are concerned.

All of us have to deal with conscience. A conscienceless person is underdeveloped or mentally ill. We struggle with our own, but as parents we play a very influential part in the shaping of our children's conscience. In Chapter 8 we shall examine what conscience is and how it is developed. We shall see some ways in which we as parents influence its development in our children.

8

Informing Their Developing Conscience

What Conscience Is

ONSCIENCE is the still, small voice of whatever God to whom it has been exposed. It does not necessarily have to have a God for reference. It could be the standards of its culture or its codes of morality. The word itself is a combination of other words meaning *with knowledge*. Conscience will operate with whatever knowledge it has. This helps to explain why there are so many different ideas of right and wrong and so many people whose consciences hurt them when other people's do not.

If we have been taught that it is wrong to dance, our conscience will hurt us if we dance. If we have been taught that it is not wrong, then we may dance with no voice from conscience disturbing us. If we have been taught that we ought to feed people who are hungry, we cannot see people go hungry without our conscience hurting us. Conscience operates both on an "ought" and "ought not" basis, but in any case the oughts and ought nots depend upon the frame of reference that has been used to establish them.

Religion is most frequently associated with conscience in our Western world where people are taught that God says this is right and that is wrong. It is not difficult for them to believe that it is God's voice reminding them when, though they ought to do right, they do wrong. In our country there are many different kinds of religious beliefs with many different concepts of God and many different standards of right and wrong. In the three major faiths in our country— Protestantism, Catholicism, and Judaism—the Ten Commandments are held in esteem. Even though there may be general agreement with respect to such principles for group living as those suggested in the Ten Commandments, there is some difference in their interpretation and application.

If children and young people are taught that it is wrong to wear clothes that show any of the body from the neck to the ankles, they will wear clothes that cover the body from the neck to the ankles or their conscience will hurt them. If they have been taught that it is wrong to wear jewelry of any kind, they will not wear jewelry or their conscience will hurt them. If people have been taught that only those who believe as we do are right, their conscience will hurt them if they suspect that maybe other people who do not believe quite as we do, may also be right.

The Role of Morality

It is the same story with respect to morality. Whatever children and young people are taught in their family or within the cultural group to which they belong will establish their sanctions and their taboos as far as morality goes. If they are taught that it is wrong to lie, their conscience may hurt them when they do. But if they are also taught that it is not necessarily wrong to lie to people outside the family, then their conscience will not hurt them when and if they lie to outsiders. If people are taught that the ends are more important than the means, then their conscience is not likely to hurt them regardless of what means they have to use to obtain the end.

Those of us with one frame of reference for conscience may find it difficult to understand how others with a different background could possibly live that way without their conscience hurting them. We simply do not realize that they have a different frame of reference for conscience. Sometimes we are so naive as to assume that they have the same frame of reference that we have. As a consequence their behavior becomes completely bewildering. One of the best ways to understand anybody's behavior is to find out what the frame of reference is for his conscience.

In the very beginning, children are completely dependent upon their parents for the determination of right and wrong. "Mamma says," or "Daddy says," is the external conscience of the child precisely because the child is dependent. When an older child begins to think for itself, it may want to construct its own frame of reference for what is good or bad, right or wrong, true or false. This happens most obviously at the same time that the young person is striving in every way for independence. But the unsureness and insecurity of the young person at this time in life is clearly revealed by the transference of dependence from parents to age mates of its own peer group.

The peer group now becomes the source of authority. Whatever the peer group thinks is right may be accepted as right. Whatever it thinks is wrong may be accepted as wrong. If the peer group is too far off from what parents think is right and wrong the young person may be thrown into considerable inner conflict because of the struggle with conscience. Whether parents win out, or the group wins, or the young person gradually establishes a frame of reference for conscience of his own will depends upon the growing strength of the self in the young person across the years. The dependent either hang on to mother and father or their age mates for anchorage and never grow up. Many adults are still in this stage of maturation. Some have substituted the church for mother and father.

Small children have to be told not to steal this particular object or that particular thing. They cannot comprehend the significance of respect for the property of others. Young people, many of them, have to have a list of commandments, ten or more. They have not yet grasped the significance of the kinds of attitudes and feelings toward one's self and others upon which these commandments rest.

The Influence of the God Concept

The highest and most powerful principle among all those thus far discerned by man, is that of an unconditional caring concern, spoken of most frequently as the love of God. Of course, this depends upon the God concept; and man has not been accused of making God in his own image without some grounds for the accusation. Those who are guilty and hostile by nature tend to have a God of justice and vengeance. Those who are suspicious and fearful tend to have a God who is a Celestial Policeman with whom one can deal or for whom one watches out. Their conscience will be shaped accordingly.

When children grow up and begin to go to school they meet children from other homes. They may be immediately in conflict over what is right and what is wrong. For the rest of their lives they will be in conflict with some of their fellows because of the many frames of reference. Parents will need to be careful how they handle a child's bewilderment and frustration because of this conflict. Parents have been rejected later by their own grown children because of the absolute and authoritarian manner in which they dealt with it. Others have been considered untrustworthy as sources for counsel because of their lack of certainty about anything.

Fear and Hostility

When too much is expected of children, or too harsh discipline is applied, fear and hostility are inevitable. Children are made to feel inferior, inadequate, incompetent, and unworthy. They may withdraw into loneliness which turns into illness, or they may become quite aggressive and turn into delinquents. Conscience is so shaped in the lives of some people that it operates on the basis of fear and they can become quite hostile in their righteousness. Envy and resentment can influence conscience. History records no viciousness and cruelty so great as that induced and condoned by a distorted religious conscience.

Faith and Friendliness

When a child, a young person, or an adult grows strong across the years and has adequate faith in himself, he is likely to have faith in others. This is the ground for friendliness. Of course, there are many substitutes. There is a kind of friendliness that is extended when we want to use somebody or something they have, or get them to do something for us. There is a kind of friendliness that we show when people have money and we want to share it or think we can get some of it. There is a kind of friendliness we extend when there is a possibility of becoming more popular because of it or more powerful socially or politically. A psychologist has said that a friend is a person who meets my needs. I would agree for the years of childhood and youth. With adult maturity, a friend is a person who needs and to whom I may give. In either case the relationship requires faith. Fear would thwart and destroy.

It has been said that faith in God is directly related to faith in man; but both operate through faith in oneself. This principle has been observed many times across history, as in those famous words of Shakespeare: "This above all: to thine own self be true, and it must follow, as the night the day, thou canst not then be false to any man." They are very close to the words of a sometimes badly misunderstood young man of centuries ago: "Love thy neighbor as thyself."

Conscience and Obedience

As parents we want our children to obey us, because we know what is best. When they become young people we may still want them to obey us, for the sake of our own ego, but they have long since proved to us that we do not always know what is best. The more unsure we are, the more absolute we are likely to be in declaring that we are sure. If we accomplish our job as parents, we shall want them sooner or later to depend on themselves. We must help them in the establishment of the kind of inner guide which we call conscience and which they must obey if they ever become independent.

We start out providing the discipline for our children and end up, if we are successful, watching them discipline themselves. This would be easy for most of us to take, if the frame of reference remained the same. What disturbs us is that at the same time they are learning to be responsible, to become their own authority, to discipline themselves, they have been establishing a new frame of reference for themselves. To whatever degree it differs from ours we are made anxious if not actually disturbed. If we think we are absolutely right, then they are wrong.

Just as we have to let them go in other respects, as they grow up and assume responsibility for their own lives, so must we let them go with respect to their development of a religious philosophy of life, a frame of reference for morality, and the kind of conscience which emerges through it and because of it. We may still fulfill our responsibility if we are able to love them, even if we think they are wrong. In the words of my grandfather, "there ought to be a law" requiring people to reach the place where they could agree to disagree without being disagreeable before they were permitted to become parents.

When Parents Violate Conscience

We have been confronted with some very terrible misuses of the words "love," "loyalty," and "respect." Some parents have based the definition of those words upon a child's or young person's agreement with them or adherence to what they felt to be right. If the young person develops any idea different from that of the parent, then this is considered proof of lack of love, of disloyalty, or lack of respect. If children have been taught that love, loyalty, and respect are equated to submission to parental authority, then they may grow on into adulthood and be in a state of conflict because of a conscience which demands that they adhere even though parents have been dead several years. This gives rise to the observation that some parents may be more dangerous dead than alive.

We tend to revere the dead. When a loved one passes

away, then all our own shortcomings and failures and omissions load us with quite a weight of guilt; and conscience may carry an extra load. If parents have succeeded in making themselves permanently dominant, then they may continue to live their grown children's lives for them from the grave. Admiration, indeed identification, with the parent may be so strong as to prevent the emergence of the individual self of the child. This is the worst kind of domination. Sooner or later, if we are successful as parents and discharge our responsibility, we shall turn our children loose, even at, or especially at, the point of the continuing development and functioning of their own conscience.

Influence of Conscience in Marriage

Since all young people who enter marriage come from a background where some form of right and wrong was accepted and taught, and since in most instances there is some slight variation, if not a very great deal of difference, between these frames of reference, there can be pangs of conscience in marriage. A husband may propose or do that which his wife cannot accept without her conscience hurting. She may propose what her husband does not want or cannot accept because he is going to stick by his conscience. There need be no complete destruction of individuality and independence in marriage; but sufficient unity of life in general, including frames of reference for conscience, seems to be important.

This is one of the strongest reasons for caution against interfaith marriage. Parents in general are remiss at the point of helping their children to understand the many significances of interfaith marriage. Difference in faith will not mean a different way of looking at certain things, but a certain way of looking at all things. Different religious backgrounds mean different consciences. What one must demand because of conscience, the other may not be able to comply with because of conscience.

Adjustment is possible through compromise for those to whom compromise is possible without too severe a violation of conscience. Conversion may resolve the conflict, provided that it is a genuine religious experience. The trouble is that most so-called conversions induced by motivations outside the religious life itself create an artificial experience, and young people proceed under an illusion that conscience has been changed. If it is a genuine religious experience of conversion, conscience will change. But if it is only an attempted conversion, motivated by the desire to eliminate the interfaith aspects of the marriage, the converting party may discover later that conscience has only been rationalized, not changed.

Parents can be of great service to their young people if they will discuss the matter of interfaith marriage with them. They may persuade their young people to talk with teachers, ministers, priests, rabbis, or whoever might be helpful in order to become insightful and understanding beyond their preconceptions and opinions. With adherents of many faiths mixed socially in our public education system and with the freedom to date according to desire that is granted many of our youth, a couple may fall in love before they know that there is any great religious difference. Their love may cause them to want to marry in spite of the interfaith problem. The young, especially, are led to believe by their love, that because they are in love, religious differences will not really matter or that their love will enable them to solve them.

Some psychiatrists point out that falling in love across religious lines, as well as other "lines" may be an expression of unconscious rebellion against parents. The defiance represented in such a marriage may be accompanied by the desire to punish parents. It is not easy to determine motivations, but those of us whose children become involved in relationships which might lead to mixed marriages would do well to seek professional consultation.

The one thing that we should remember is that conscience is cultivable. If it ever crystallizes we stop growing and developing as far as our knowledge of right and wrong, good and bad, God and the Universe are concerned. There are altogether too many adults with infantile consciences, or at least consciences appropriate to childhood. Adolescent conscience is adequate for adolescence, but it plagues all too many beyond those years. Conscience, like love, should be changing and growing and developing all the way through life.

One of the things related to conscience is money. It is involved in all marriages. In our monetary economy no one can escape dealing with it. Some people in pointing to what causes trouble in marriage put the finger on money first. We are very much concerned with it, or about it. How our children relate to it later in their marriages is partly determined by how we help our children come to understand its significance. In this next chapter we shall observe some things about our opportunity and responsibility as parents with money.

9

Providing
Opportunities
to
Learn
About
Money

COUNSELORS FIND that financial problems are very prominent among those causing trouble in marriage. In view of the number of homes that are lost each year because of inability to continue the payments and the number of pieces of furniture and appliances that are repossessed, it would appear that quite a number of people are in trouble with money matters. If you listen to people as they talk, there does not seem to be anything in the world that could not be taken care of if they just had a little more money.

This attitude is not surprising since we have developed a monetary value system whereby more than things are measured for worth by money. It is not surprising when we recognize that in our efforts to make an impression upon others and achieve a status satisfying to ourselves, we find money a very powerful instrument. It is so important that some people will do almost anything for it. Always there is the refrain, "if we just had a little more money."

Most of the research suggests that it is not the amount of money that people have after they get past the subsistence level: it is the way they get it and use it that matters. The specialists put their finger on management as the chief cause of the trouble with finances in marriage. Perhaps it is because people are not so businesslike about financial affairs connected with the family as they are with those connected with their business. Many a partnership would break up in a hurry if one partner treated the other partner as a great many husbands treat their wives or vice versa. But what we are concerned about here is how to deal with our children in such manner as to give them the best opportunity to learn how to manage the money we give them.

Children and Allowances

One way to provide money for our children is by an allowance. There is no general agreement as to when it ought to begin and how much it ought to be. Some parents dish out the pennies by the time the children can walk; others, nickels and dimes; still others, quarters, depending on the digits in their bank account. Some wait for their children to start to school. Others follow the plan of providing only enough money for candy or nonessentials. Some will begin to include school lunches, certain student fees, admission price for cultural and athletic events, and so on. Usually children are not introduced to the relation of clothing to money until they have reached the upper grades and high school. When children are given allowances only for the fun and frivolity side of life, they may not learn much about where money comes from and how to manage it. They may remain dependent upon parents for financial survival even after marriage.

Some parents believe in helping a child begin to get the feel of the significance of money by introducing him to work for pay at an early age. Since urban homes do not have many chores by comparison with farm homes, some parents let their children do housework or yard work and pay them for it. There is considerable debate over the wisdom of this. It may destroy children's feeling of shared responsibility in matters concerning the family. It threatens their willingness to work at home without pay.

The Idea of Shares

Some parents have given a little different psychological twist to the money provided their children. Instead of calling it an allowance they call it shares. The theory is that children as members of the family should share in the father's pay check just as the mother does. In this latter instance there is more likely to be some form of family council. Children are introduced to some understanding of father's efforts which bring financial returns and of the relation of the family's needs and fun to this income.

In some families when children reach the junior high school age or a little older they may be allowed the experience of shopping with father or mother along to guide. The stores are always full of children, but not many of them are actually examining the prices and checking the labels for weights and other information important if people are to become intelligent buyers. Here and there you will find a parent who is encouraging a child to participate. Such a parent will very likely sooner or later turn a proportion of the shopping over to this child.

One possible reason why there is so little of this may be because parents in general are poor buyers themselves. Findings from Consumer Research indicate an unfortunate lack of knowledge and skill in the use of money. Many families would have more goods if they knew how to use the money they have. There are signs of interest on the part of some teachers, but consumer education is not yet recognized as a significant offering in the curriculum of our schools.

The manufacturers, distributors, and retailers have employed the best psychologists they can find to help them sell their products. These psychologists make a study of the weaknesses, the frustrations, the unfulfilled desires of people. They spend money and time discovering how people may be induced to buy whether they need or can afford to do so. They endeavor to use all the knowledge of human nature that they can come by in order to persuade consumers to purchase. They have developed hidden persuaders, devices to influence and exploit the unconscious. A long time ago a slogan emerged which correctly describes the situation: "Let the buyer beware." But where are the psychologists who are helping the consumer to understand and resist the psychological persuasions of the sellers? Some co-operatives have been formed to attempt to control exploitation. Consumer Research is one national organization attempting to counteract high-pressure salesmanship, the "hard sell." But how many parents make use of resources such as this?

Where parents let their young people accompany them on buying excursions and teach them how to shop for quality as well as price, young people emerge fairly well prepared for responsible independence in their use of money as they move on toward adulthood. But this takes time, and we are impatient with time for competent parenthood.

Some parents will include their own children in discussions which involve financial planning for the future. Some parents turn the bookkeeping over to one of the older children for a series of months. This one has the responsibility of working out payments for bills at the end of the month and advising all other members of the family concerning the state of the treasury.

Young people are intrigued with the handling of finances when they are given responsibility and a little authority. Sometimes young people of high school age ask their parents to help them learn how the income tax is figured. This is really evidence of sincere interest!

Child's Money—Our Value System

Going back to the early allowances, children and parents are frequently in conflict because of differing value systems. A mother told me not long ago that she gave her child some money to spend at the dime store. She could hardly bear to see him spend it on the first object that captured his fancy. She kept wanting to caution him to hold on to it until he could look at some other things. She was wise enough, when he saw other things that he wanted, to help him understand that because he had already spent his money, he did not have it to buy anything else.

In a little while the child began of his own accord to hang on to his money until he had looked at several other things and then to make a selection. There was always pressure for more. His mother struggled to resist his attempts through anger to get it. She had to withstand whining and begging, but it was not long before her son would cover quite a bit of the toy department before he made a selection. He had learned that this was the limit of his resources. There was no more forthcoming. It was a wiser procedure to look around before he spent his money.

The Importance of Attitudes

Sometimes parents complain about the silly things their children have bought with money. This usually means a difference in the value systems. Things on a counter do not look the same to a child as to parents. Of course, children do not have the experience and knowledge with which to discriminate between values and durability, but one thing we ought to try to keep in mind, is that a child has a right to its own value system. The parent has no right to superimpose his own on the child. There may be discussion between them, there may be comparisons, there may be experiences in which the child is helped to learn the difference, but the child must be respected as a person. If any money is going to be given at all, the parent should respect the child's right to use it as he pleases.

One trouble with us in dealing with our children when it comes to money is that we assign the responsibility but do not turn over to them the appropriate authority that should go with it. We want to hang on to that and make final decisions ourselves. It will cost us less, but the child will not learn so much. We can save money, but we may not save the child.

Some parents take attitudes toward their children's use of money which might be expressed in the story of the father who said to his son, "I am not going to let you go near the water until you show me you know how to swim." The ridiculousness of that attitude is apparent at first glance. Principles are similar with respect to a child who is learning how to use money. There will be some splashing around and struggling in the process. It will cost us, but we fool ourselves into thinking that they will learn about money in good time and that in the meantime it is our responsibility to make sure they do not waste it. We can control that by the amount we give them. They have the right to waste it and we have the responsibility to see that they take the consequences. They will learn from that. This is an interesting attitude since most adults are quite willing to pay whatever it costs for whatever material services or experiences seem to be worth it. We seem reluctant, however, to pay the cost of a child's learning how to use money.

Youth and Gainful Employment

Some older children, having discovered something of the significance of money, begin to hunt for odd jobs outside the home from which to secure it. Clubs and organizations which use them as solicitors encourage this. The newsboy is famous as an ideal of the young business man. By the time they have reached high school many boys and girls have secured part-time work or full-time summer jobs. They make some of the money they use for their own clothes and their school expenses. Many of them contribute to family resources. One of the risks is that having learned how to use money and gotten a taste of its returns they may lose their interest in further education and jump into the job world before they are trained well enough to secure the kind of jobs and promotion that would move them on up the economic ladder. Young people need counsel from parents with respect to their acquisition and use of money all the way into adulthood.

Like Parent—Like Son or Daughter

When parents are not too good in managing their financial affairs and are at each other's throats every time the monthly bills come around, a feeling of considerable insecurity may be superimposed upon children. Some parents hold up discussion of finances until children have gone to bed. Others expose them to the full blast of their frustration and anger. We are influencing our children and young people by the manner in which we handle our finances and by our attitudes and feelings about it. We include them in experiences that enable them to learn and gradually to assume responsibility, thereby contributing to their management of money, or we block them from it and keep them dependent. We hold them back so that they reach adulthood too immature to handle the demands as far as the management of money is concerned.

Children quickly discern by the importance given it by parents how valuable money is in any home. Where it is worshiped as the key to status, children are impressed by its significance. Where it is the cause of all the fighting between mother and father and of their lack of adequate supplies across the growing-up years, children may be influenced in a measure to overevaluate its significance and cause them to make it the most important goal in their life.

Where parents are stingy or miserly, children may be led into deceitful ways of securing it and hidden ways of using it. Where parents are concerned about human values and the greater significance of the worth of personality resources which are developing across the years, money may fall into place in its proper proportion under such perspective. Children from such homes usually remain masters of money. They make it their servant and it serves them well. Where parents are not successful in relating money to the rest of life, children may be trained to worship it. They usually turn out to be slaves of it.

The traditions still dominate in some homes, and men think they are the only ones who should handle the money since they are the ones who make it. Mother is placed in the unhappy position of having to ask for it whenever she needs it. A little is doled out to the children here and there according to the father's estimate of their need or merit.

In those homes where the mother has become aggressive and dominant across the years, where father is what is called "passive submissive," the finances may be handled altogether by her. Children observe that father brings home the pay check and turns it over to mother and mother pays the bills. She dishes it out to everyone, including father, according to her judgment. In other homes the money may be placed in a joint checking account. Children observe father and mother planning for responsibility and sharing in the dispensing of funds. Either father or mother may handle the books. It depends upon who is better at keeping accounts. Children note that decisions are arrived at jointly. Sex does not determine who handles finances.

Long before adulthood young people should be introduced to the significance of insurance for the home, for the automobile, and for members of the family. In some homes investments may be included in the education of the young. Not much is offered in our public school system yet, and so the family still remains an important educational influence with respect to financial affairs.

A father took his thirteen-year-old daughter to the bank and established a checking account for her. He induced her to talk with the cashier about how to handle the checkbook. When the cashier suggested that the father would take care of any overdrawals the father calmly stated that he would not. The cashier was smart enough to catch on and said that in that instance perhaps they had better go and talk with the vice-president. The father introduced his daughter to this official and indicated that he was establishing a checking account for her. The vice-president chuckled and said he guessed that if there was an overdrawal the father would take care of it. This time the daughter said that her daddy would not. The vice-president sensed the situation and proceeded to inform the girl about how such matters are handled. From there they went to the window where she would get her statement at the end of the month. They spent some time in the bank, and the daughter was introduced to various people from whom she could secure information if she needed it.

The father then took his daughter to the managers of three stores in town and informed them that he was establishing a checking account for her. He stated that he would appreciate their honoring her checks. Two of the three managers made the same remark about father taking care of checks that bounced, but the daughter replied in both instances that he would not and there would be no overdrawals. She was right. There were none.

She got in over her head, however, in borrowing money from her friends. Her father let her flounder, refusing to advance any money toward the next month's deposit. She gradually realized that borrowing money was a little like writing a check on money you didn't have in the bank. At any rate it would be taken out of next month's deposit. Whatever she might want to use that for would be impossible.

The Use of Money—a Personality Expression

There are many motives for the use of money. A man feels inferior. If he can buy what the psychologist working for the advertisers tell him will make him superior to most everyone else he may feel all right through this compensation. It may be an electric razor, a kind of shirt, a certain automobile, a house in a restricted area, but whatever it is that he buys serves to cover up, to make up for his feeling of inferiority.

A woman may feel that she is not a very attractive personality. She may feel that she is not beautiful, and so much of her money may go for clothes and cosmetics. Characteristically, girls who do not date much want more clothes than those who do.

A man feels that he does not really amount to much. Nobody pays any attention to him. If he can get money they will pay attention to him. He needs power to feel important. Money is power. He makes the mistake of assuming that he is worth a lot simply because he has a lot. He is fooled by the attitude of people toward him because of his money. He thinks that they regard him when it is mainly his money that they regard.

Some people need friends. Not knowing how or not having the resources to *be* friends they set out to get money and buy friends. Such friends are not worth the name of friend, as many a person has discovered who suddenly lost his money. A great many things are available with money, but what really matters is not always purchasable. False love and affection can be bought. Pretentious sex is for sale. But the real thing is available only in kind. Love and affection can secure love and affection that is real. Companionship is its own creator. The kind purchasable with money is cheap, deceitful, and uncertain.

A husband in a marriage where he is sole provider can use money as a whip or bargaining instrument with his wife just as she can use sex. A wife can attempt to get revenge by deliberate extravagance. It is very true that money talks. The important thing is what it says. Sometimes in our getting and spending money it says that we are weak and cannot manage our own impulses. It may say that I am a cheat. It may say that I am dominated by moods. Sometimes money says that I envy. It may say that I feel worthless. It may say that I am angry and want to punish. Money sometimes says that I love, but it can say that I hate. Sometimes it says simply that I am a poor manager.

Money may say that I am sensitive to the needs of others. It may say that I understand and want to help. It may say that I am strong and can be depended upon. We get and spend money according to our needs. In our use of money we express ourselves. That is another reason why it is so important that we pay so much attention to the little selves of our children. That is why we must be concerned with the responsible independence of our young people. That is why we must be sure that they get what they need for the development of the resources that make our children persons. In dealing with them in ways to stimulate their maturation we are determining, to great measure, how they will think and feel about and use money. Since financial problems are listed high, many times first, among causes of trouble in marriage, we may see that this really means that people express their immaturities and inadequacies in handling money. Where things go well their use of money expresses their competency and maturity. In influencing our children to grow up we are preparing them to handle money matters in marriage.

In the adult world most money comes from work. With the exaggerated importance of money in our culture there is a mad scramble to get it. The pace of our world has been stepped up. Even with fewer working hours in the week, the pressure is increased. Tension mounts. Work, like any other virtue, can be overdone. We may need to learn to relax. In the next chapter we shall examine both work and play, their relation to each other, and our role as parents in helping our children learn to use them. In so doing, we are preparing them for marriage.

10

Teaching
Them
to
Work
and
Play

All Work and No Play

A LL WORK and no play" may not only make Johnny a
very dull boy; it will make him an unhealthy one. Play
is as essential as food to growth and development in childhood. Children, because they are children, cannot manage
the adult world and must retreat into the unreal world of
imagination in order to have a sense of competency and
worthfulness of their own. This is their world of play. They
develop muscles and skills, they develop relationships and
confidence in the process. Many times they work out their
frustrations and they express their anger. They do a great
deal of normal growing just through play.

Recently we have begun to recognize the significance of
play for children and adults. Tensions are so great and the
pace so fast that play has become a necessity for mental and

physical health. An archer's bow that is kept strung up will lose its power. Any human being that gives himself entirely to work will lose his power too. A whole new profession is developing in the field of recreation which is guided play. Many other jobs and vocations are emerging in the field of play as a result of the increasing amount of our leisure time.

There is much conflict in some homes over the children's play or over the play of a father or mother. Somebody thinks that somebody else plays too much or feels that he never has any time to play and resents whatever play the other enjoys. Working *and* playing come within the arena of family adjustments. Parents have an important part in the cultivation of some balance on the part of children in these experiences.

All Play and No Work

All play and no work would probably make Johnny not only dull, but useless, if not a dangerous boy. After a while a person gets bored with nothing but play. Boredom is usually found in the background of some of the kinds of antipersonal and antisocial behavior that we classify as crime and delinquency. Children can be greatly helped if, as they grow older, they are led to understand the significance of both work *and* play. They are happiest when parents help them to engage in both, doing some of each with them.

Time was when work was an inescapable necessity. It was the means of survival. It took about all the time we had. It is still important in providing for our needs, but it goes far beyond that and provides for comfort and luxury. It is more than a necessity. It is a privilege. But something has happened to it in this country of ours that we might well examine. We have witnessed the development of the idea that we should try to get as much pay for as little work as we can. When we get a job we should act as if we knew what it was all about even though we might have no training for it. We act as if we thought that anything we can get by with is all right.

There is a noticeable lack of pride in good workmanship. Pressure seems to be in the direction of getting it ready as fast as possible and making it look presentable, whether or not it will stand much stress and demonstrate much durability. We are helped along these lines with the development of a national attitude sometimes characterized as our "economy of obsolesence." Parental attitudes, whether they reflect these attitudes or their opposite, are quite influential in shaping the attitudes of children and young people toward work.

Children used to be introduced to work around the home. Some still are, but they are inclined to resent having to do the kind of work that parents do not like to do. They are quick to sense whether this is the case. If it is, we may be confronted with a considerable amount of resistance on their part. Since at any time work is bound to interfere with play, we can expect normal resistance anyway. Children are not yet sufficiently mature to discipline themselves to work. They must therefore have parental discipline if they are to be involved in work even to a reasonable degree.

When Parents and Children Play Together

If parenthood is to be discharged anywhere near appropriately, parents should play occasionally with their own children. This includes every age from infancy until the time that they leave home as responsible young adults. This does not mean that parents ought to be included in all the play in which children or young people engage. Nothing irks young people so much as to have dad or mother come plunging in when they are playing with their own age mates, regress to an adolescent level, and attempt to be one of the gang. Sometimes this is all right, but the invitation had better come from the young people. Young people are sensitive about their play and about the intrusion of elders into it.

Many a fine relationship between a father and son has developed and been maintained across the years through hunting, fishing, or some similar activity. Even so, there comes a time when his son will want to engage in the same outdoor activity with those of his own age and father will not be included. If father understands this, his feelings are not so likely to be hurt. If he does not understand, he will feel left out and his reaction is likely to make it embarrassing for his son. He may insist on going along or restrict his son's going with his friends.

Many mothers and daughters have experienced a great deal of the fellowship and fun of play across the years. The same principles govern their relationship too. Parents have been involved in their children's venturing into the world of work, carrying newspapers, cutting lawns, or doing whatever odd jobs they have secured that brought in a little pay. Decisions had to be made, approval had to be secured. Support, sometimes in the form of equipment had to be supplied. But it is not usually until high school that parents are faced with the problem of guidance when their young people face vocational choice.

The attitudes and feelings that parents have about their own work have already made an impression in the lives of the young. Sometimes this is supportive and at other times threatening. If a child feels for any reason compelled to go ahead in the same direction as his father or his mother, there may be trouble ahead. This kind of coercion may be submitted to because of financial assistance needed to go through any kind of preparation. Resentment will build and can fester across the years.

I well remember the man who wanted to study law. His

father was a doctor and wanted him to study medicine. He would help his son through college only if he took medical training. He turned out to be one of those square pegs in a round hole. When I saw him he was halfway through life. He decided to cut down on his medical practice and attend law school. His wife understood and was supportive. Today he is a prominent lawyer. He specializes in legal matters related to the field of medicine. His story seems to have a happy ending. Many others do not.

I knew a father whose daughter wanted a college education in science. He thought such an education was for men only and refused to help her unless she would specialize in the arts. The question is not what field a young person heads toward but whether he has freedom to choose or is coerced by his parents.

Parents and Vocational Guidance

Parents who wish to help may get in touch with a high school counselor. At his suggestion they may read the most recent developments in the matter of vocational counseling. Things have changed since they were young and, unless they have taken the trouble to keep up, it is not likely that they will know of the emerging situations beyond their own jobs into which their young people may go for a vocational experience. Conferences with vocational guidance personnel on the part of the parents may put them in a better position to be of use to their own young people at home. Parents should suggest such conferences to their young adults and discuss attitudes and feelings as well as facts uncovered at home. Young people want to know how their parents think and how they feel. They do not want to be told what to do. They want the decision to be left up to them.

When a general direction is decided upon, parents should

be supportive in their encouragement of their young to secure adequate training. Here, too, the fact that their child is not just like themselves may mean a little different point of view or some difference in feeling, and the young person must be respected in his choice if the best relationships are to be cultivated.

Some financial assistance will undoubtedly be needed for the training period. There may be a need for some support during the first stages of effort in the new vocation. Until the young person has got his feet on the ground and begun to feel sure of himself in his new enterprise, parental help may be in order. But it had better be without strings, or resentment will be a good possibility on both sides.

This is particularly true in the event of a young marriage where parents are offering some help for the establishment of a home and "for getting them started." Too much help may result in the development of dependency and interfere with both ambition and independence. It could threaten pride and increase guilt. It could result in resentment because it implies inferiority. Most of us do not like being under obligation and tend not to like the persons to whom we are obligated. The fact that we are related may modify such feelings, but it could make them worse. Not enough help may actually contribute to the struggle on the part of the young, and such struggle could be more than necessary. In any event, whatever help is given ought to be *given* and not on condition that parents have a part in decisions which are to be made.

The Threat and Support of Ambition

Far back down in childhood ambition emerges principally from the drives for status. It expresses itself in the competition in which children engage in the last of the grades and on into high school. Its mainspring is a feeling of inferiority. Ambition, like all other virtues, is a virtue so long as it is not pushed to an extreme. If the compulsive need is great it may become so all-consuming as to interfere with anything like a balanced and harmonious life. Many a wife who married a man because of his ambition later found that she was alone in the world for the same reason. Her husband supplied her with all the external things she might like, but denied her the one thing that she needed most—himself. He was too busy fulfilling his ambition.

Ambition matters as such, but that toward which it is directed also matters. This is usually determined by the needs of the child and the emerging young person. If a goal is so high that it is impossible, there is likely to be no ambition to fulfill it. Or if a young person feels that the goal is all right, but he simply does not have what it takes to achieve it, there may be no ambition. Realistic goals and confidence in the self are essential if ambition is to function constructively in the life of anyone.

Children will have observed how this operated in the lives of their father and mother. We, therefore, in the fulfillment of our own ambitions in life or in our failure to do so and our frustration because of it, are educating our children in this matter. Their ambitions will affect their marriage. They may determine it.

Life Work Versus Work Life

There is a difference in work as a means to life and work as life. This was discerned centuries ago and expressed in religious language somewhat as follows: "Where your treasure is, there will your heart be also." In those days heart was the symbol for life. It was not only the center, but the pulsing extent of it. We have parallel language along the way. We have often heard, "He didn't succeed because he didn't put his heart into it." What we meant was he did not put enough interest and effort into it. He did not invest enough of his life in it.

Certainly serious, persistent, determined effort is important in the accomplishment of anything. But life is more inclusive than work. Anyone who buries himself in his work is burying his life. Those who have invested their life altogether in work resist the approach of retirement as if it were the end of life. For all too many it is the end.

A friend of mine, a machinist, resisted retirement so strongly that they had to eject him forcibly from his job. He threw his tools away, several hundred dollars' worth, and retreated into self-pity and aloneness. He refused to go anywhere or see anyone. He made an attempt upon his life because he considered himself worthless and hated himself for it. We finally succeeded in persuading him to talk with his minister, who in turn persuaded him to see a psychiatrist. After more than a year he purchased new tools and began to use them to help friends of his. Soon he had a small private business going.

It became quite amusing to see how he operated. Since he was retired he refused to follow any regular schedule. He quit whenever he wanted to. He would close up and go fishing at the rise of the barometer. Friends got used to him and shrugged their shoulders. They expected their work to be finished sooner or later and didn't worry about it. Neither did he.

In helping our children to learn the significance of work we should help them to understand its relation to the rest of life. It is self-defeating when it becomes an end within itself. As long as it is a means to other ends, it may be constructive. Those other ends ought to be the fullest development of personality and the extension of personality to others. Our attitudes toward our work are profoundly significant in our experience with life.

In too many homes mother raises the children because father is working all the time. Or the children run the streets because mother is also working and no adequate arrangement has been made for them. All work and no play can make parents pretty dull people. In some homes it is the father or mother who is playing most of the time. Too much of this can wreck things too. Here again we suggest that work and play are both personality expressions. Our needs are revealed by what we do and how we do it. If we are influencing our children in such manner as to help them develop well-balanced personalities work can be used in the process. Their relationship to it all through their life will be evidence of it.

Work as Personality Expression

There is a man so selfish that it shows up in both his work and his play. He thinks he should be free to go out nights with the boys and bowl or play cards or drink, but he is greatly angered at the suggestion that his wife join some of her friends in having fun for an evening. Children are keen little observers and they size things up pretty well. They are thrown into considerable conflict wherever they see distortion of unfairness in the relationship between father and mother. In today's tight society of urban life they are exposed to other parents and have a chance for comparison which sometimes helps and sometimes threatens.

Fathers and mothers do not always have the same value system, as we have already noted; among other reasons, because one is male and the other is female. It is unlikely that the average woman will have the same appreciation of the worth of a sixteen-gauge shotgun as the average man. It is certain that the average man will not place the same value on a woman's hat as almost any woman might. Whatever is involved by way of equipment that costs money for either work or play can be a cause of controversy in marriage. Some men will spend fabulous sums of money for garden equipment when a wife feels that the whole yard could be taken care of at one-tenth the cost. She doesn't realize that this investment is in play as much as it is in work. Most men have no idea in the world about the financial involvements of a normal woman's wardrobe. They just explode when the bills come in.

One area of precious memories for most people is that of the work and the play that they did together as a family when they were children. Listen to them as they reminisce when they get together as adults in a family reunion. They will dwell upon the strenuous exertions and the strain of the work in which they engaged along with father. They would not go through it again, but they wouldn't take anything for the experience. They will laugh hilariously at the recollections of the play that involved them all. Work and play build traditions which operate to strengthen family life. The happiest marriages emerge from the experiences of a couple whose backgrounds have given them ample opportunity to discover the significance of both work and play and achieve some balance between them according to their needs in life for health and happiness.

Finally, we all have to learn to face reality and deal with it successfully. We as parents have been struggling to do it for some time. As parents we have the problem of helping our children to do it. In the next chapter we shall examine some of the methods and obstacles confronting us and our children. We shall see how some people try to escape from failure in dealing with reality. We shall see more ways toward success.

11

Encouraging
Them
to
Deal
with
Reality

The Child's World of Fantasy

CHILDREN live a considerable part of their lives in the unreal world of fantasy. The real world of adults around them is too overwhelming. They lack the knowledge and the strength with which to cope with it. A wise providence apparently planned it so that they could retreat from this real world into a world of their own making. In the world of imagination we can control all the elements. It is a very satisfying world because children can shape it the way they want it.

A great amount of anguish, anger, and frustration exists among adults because they cannot shape the real world just the way they want it. They have never developed the resources with which to deal with it as it is, and they are forever trying to make everything over, including people, to suit their own desires. There is not much chance for them to be happy or for anyone very close to them to be happy under these circumstances.

We have all seen children at play. Imagination is a great part of it. I remember hearing my four-year-old daughter in animated conversation with playmates. Being curious, I approached to see what they were doing. To my surprise there was only my daughter with a tea table set with toy dishes, but evidently surrounded by several imaginary guests. She was addressing herself to each of them in turn and responding to their silent communication as if they were really there. In her imagination they were. She could see them. She was having a wonderful time with them. She welcomed me into her wonderful world of fantasy and introduced me to her friends one by one.

Many of us have found out that we can discover surprising things about ourselves if we will listen to our children playing house. They are great little imitators and as they play the role of the father or the mother, they will act out what has impressed them in our relationships with them. One of the most amusing cartoons that I recall seeing was that of a little boy and girl in their parents' clothing. She was suggesting that they kiss each other and he said, "Okay, but we have to fight first."

The childhood world of imagination is fraught with dangers as well as pleasures. If the child's real experience is one of safety and security, this threat is at a minimum. If the child's real experience is fraught with anxiety and apprehension, then even its world of imagination can be bordered by the dark forests of the foreboding and threatening. In our dealing with our children, we help to make their world of unreality something of a reflection of their real experiences with us. If we are warm, accepting parents, fun to be with, and sharing some of our excitement with them, or providing opportunity for them to experience new adventure, then their world of fantasy becomes an extension of this happiness. If we are too busy and too harsh in dealing with them, if we criticize and condemn more than we praise and support, then it is more fun to get away from us and dream of parents that are the sort they would like to have.

Amid the raging arguments over the effect of TV and radio on children some parents have noted the accumulation of research dealing with the question. The gist of it seems to suggest that effects on any particular child depend upon the emotional condition of that child. If the real world of its home and of its relation to its parents is a safe, secure, and happy world in the main, then the violence and threatening on the screen seems to be unreal and in the same category as fairy tales. If, however, the child's world is full of conflict and violence or the threat of violence and is conducive to the feeling that the world is an unsafe and insecure place full of dangers and threats, the screen may have marked effect on the child. That which is appearing on the screen is too nearly like parts of the child's real world and is accepted as reality.

The Regression of Adults to Childhood

It is not uncommon to see adults regress to childhood in their behavior when they are facing crisis. Someone throws a tantrum like a three-year-old. Someone else expresses insecurity and anxiety through the tensions of chain smoking. Still another attempts to escape or compensate from some situation in which he feels inferior or inadequate by running back to infancy and taking to the bottle. The only thing that is missing is the nipple.

Some men faced by rejection of loved ones or friends, or in the throes of self-rejection, may run back across the years and search for mother's breast, the only safe and secure and satisfying experience they can recall. On the adult level this may take the form of sexual promiscuity. Still other adults are in need of more financial resources than they are able to secure by legitimate means and resort to childish efforts to secure something for nothing. Either they steal or they resort to gambling.

The world of imagination and fantasy very often constitutes a sanctuary for adults who feel too threatened. If across the years we do not help our children to cope with the real world as they grow up in it, they will frequently seek this sanctuary in efforts to hide or to make up for inadequacy or failure.

I remember my first date in high school. I was so self-conscious and embarrassed that I could not say a word. We went to the movie and that was a considerable relief. I could sit there for two hours without having to say anything. When the movie was over I took her home and left her there with a great sense of elation at having had a date and great relief because it was over.

Fantasy as Compensation for Inadequacy

I was acuately aware of my awkwardness and lack of social skill, so I daydreamed another date with the same girl, only now everything went along fine. This was so much fun that I dreamed up a date with a blonde in the class and the girl I was really interested in was around and aware and very jealous. In my imagination I was really a "Don Juan." In later years I recognized this as simply a retreat into the unreal world of imagination in an effort to compensate for not very much competency in the real world of social relationships. I also found out that Don Juan was not a great lover, but a man-size boy who was always looking for a mother.

My first uneasiness was not so great as to keep me from venturing again; and so, after a number of dates, I began to feel more relaxed and at home in the social situation. In direct proportion to my growing confidence I found that I had less of a tendency to retreat into the world of imagination.

Here was a man who could never hold a job for very long. He needed status, was forever borrowing money with which to try to establish himself on a level which he wanted for himself and his family, but he simply did not have the personality resources with which to be successful in any of the number of jobs that he secured. Every time he came home after having been fired, it was always the company's fault or that of someone in particular who had a grudge against him. It was usually the man he envied and wanted to be like. His way of trying to achieve equality was to chop the other man down and in the process build himself up. To hear him tell it, he was not only better than average, but always going to do something really great. It was just around the corner. It was within the foreseeable future, but it never materialized. He was one of the most pathetic men conceivable. He lived almost as much of the time in the unreal world of his own imagination as do children.

The Common Need to Escape

This is not an uncommon experience for us all. There are moments when we need to escape. We may do it by plunging into the pages of a magazine or a book. We may go to a movie. We may watch television. We may take a vacation. We may simply daydream. We may sleep. There is nothing wrong with all this until, and unless, we begin to use it as a substitute for doing what we are supposed to do.

We all need to be recognized. If we cannot secure recognition through our achievement in the real world, we will retreat into the realm of imagination and become heroes and heroines in order to feed and satisfy our need for recognition. We all want adventure. If life is too dull and monotonous we retreat into some effort to supply our need for adventure through the realm of imagination and fantasy. Many a woman who longs for romance and the only thing she can recognize as love, may retreat into the unreal world of imagination through the pages of romance magazines or movies. The man whose work life is dull and unexciting may endeavor to compensate by similar excursions into books or movies of adventure.

Whether our children will need this retreat from reality after they are grown up, depends to a great measure upon how successful we are in dealing with them across their childhood years. Some parents are so impatient that they will not give a child time to learn. It is so much easier, as a mother, to do it yourself than to keep after a child until the child does it. A father says, "He can never do it right; I may as well go ahead and do it in the first place." Children of such parents are denied their right to discover themselves and to develop their own ability in dealing with the ordinary little responsibilities of life at home. They will secure a sense of adequacy or competency, if they ever get it, through the actual achievement of little tasks at school or elsewhere. The achievement of bigger tasks does not depend upon how old children are, or how much they weigh and how tall they are, nearly so much as upon whether they have been successful in the achievement of little tasks leading up to the big ones.

Yesterday Versus Today

In the farm homes of the previous century, children had a better opportunity to learn to work than those living in the cities today. They were confronted with the reality of work from the time they could toddle. Since a great deal of the work was done with the hands and its results could easily be seen, they could judge their own adequacy by their accomplishments. They learned to deal with the real world by dealing with it. Today's children have little or nothing to do with their own hands. Much of the work provided them is artificially manufactured. Their clubs and organizations and the field of athletics, their participation in drama and music seem to be the ways in which they strive to satisfy themselves that they are doing all right in the growing-up process. Considerable confusion exists between standards of measurements used by parents and those used by children and young people. In our rapidly changing society the distance between generations seems to be greater as each new generation comes along. Communication and adjustment seem more frustrating.

When we are forever making decisions for our children and young people, for fear that they might make a wrong one, we deny them the chance to learn to deal adequately with the real world. If we are too much afraid of their making mistakes, we deny them the right to learn through their own mistakes. A mother had to become ill and be taken to the hospital before her three children had a chance to learn much about housekeeping. The mother worried so much that the father promised to secure a housekeeper. The second day she was there an emergency developed in her own family and she had to leave. The father and children agreed not to tell their mother, and everything went along well. When she came home from the hospital she was surprised at how well things were going. Then she was threatened by the discovery that she was not indispensable. The father and children succeeded in convincing her that she was, as far as love and affection were concerned. But had this mother not become ill, her children would never have had the chance to learn how to work, to derive the satisfaction from doing it and to receive the praise and commendation from their father which meant so much. If we cannot stand the mess, or figure that the cost is too much, we can handicap them in their efforts to learn. We may block their chances to become competent.

Interference by Parents

Sometimes parents are greatly concerned over the retreat of children into the world of fantasy; they may try to force them to stay in the real world. This is particularly true with respect to exaggerations and misrepresentations which may appear to parents as lying. Some parents are greatly disturbed and quite threatening to their children of four and five years of age for lack of understanding of the time and circumstances in the life of a child during which such behavior is normal. Lacking enough knowledge or parental insight, parents with every good intent can violate the development of a child and frequently do so.

On the other hand, there was the father who loved to enter his children's world of fantasy and participate with them in some of their adventures. On one occasion they were on a bear hunt in the mountains. The living room furniture constituted the mountains and the father was designated by the children to be the bear. He entered into the part so enthusiastically that he became a little frightening, and his five-year-old daughter came out of her world of imagination and reminded her father that he was, after all, not a real bear. This suggests that children have their own protective devices against losing themselves in the unreal world.

A mother was confronted by a daughter who was building up quite a palace of white lies. The mother decided to engage in the game of construction along with her. The mother took her cues from the daughter and began stretching things to such an extent that after a while the little girl shook her head and said, "Now, Mommy, you know that's not so."

We can help our children most in dealing successfully with the world of reality as adults if we are concerned to help them all the way along from infancy according to their age and strength and ability. A good book for parents of young children to help them understand what seems to be the sort of behavior that may be expected of a child at different ages is the book titled *These Are Your Children* by Gladys G. Jenkins and others.

The Parents' Responsibility in Facing Reality

If we are successful in helping our young people to develop a reasonably fair image of themselves and a fairly good regard for themselves there will be less need for them to pretend when they grow up. They will not have to live so much of their lives as adults acting as if they were people other than the persons they really are. There is altogether too much of an attempt at imitation on the adult level. This is clear evidence of the rejection of the self as inadequate and an attempt to appear to be like someone admired or worshiped.

*   *   *   *   *

Now to summarize our thinking in the whole book: If we are successful in helping our children to become responsibly independent, to get according to their needs, they will be better able to enjoy the pleasures of giving as adults. They will not have to resort only to substitutes such as commercialized devices for excitement and adventure, and crutches such as smoking, drinking and illicit sex in order to derive the greatest satisfactions from life.

If we are successful in expressing affection and in guiding them in their understanding and experience of sex, there will be less need for their retreat into the abnormalities for satisfactions. If we have helped them adjust to difference they may more easily adjust to each other as husband and wife. If we have helped them learn to deal with frustration and disappointment, they will more easily handle these in marriage. If we have helped them see that the effects of tragedy depend on the attitude they take toward it, we may have saved their marriage, if not their lives. Their competency as adults in life, but especially in married life, depends to a great extent upon our competency as parents across the years.

Let us observe again that we are not the sole influence in the lives of our children but we are the first and perhaps the most profound influence. We have said, over and over again, that the best gift we can give our children is a good marriage, *our own*. If we are sufficiently successful and happy, we create the fair weather within which our children grow. A few storms now and then do not matter too much. But if it is all stormy weather our children may have to look to others for their models, their inspiration, and some grounds for hope.

We may be of help through instruction in guiding their growth and development in ways that will influence their experience in marriage later on. Our greatest influence, however, will be in our being the person we are as husband or wife before them all across the years.

For
Suggested
Reading

Abrahamsen, David, *The Road to Emotional Maturity* (Englewood Cliffs, N.J.: Prentice-Hall, Inc., 1958)

Baruch, Dorothy, *New Ways in Sex Education* (New York: McGraw-Hill Book Co., Inc., 1959)

Beecher, Marguerite and Willard, *Parents on the Run* (New York: Julian Press, Inc., 1955)

Blood, Robert, *Husbands and Wives* (New York: The Free Press of Glencoe, Inc., 1960)

——, *Marriage* (New York: The Free Press of Glencoe, Inc., 1962)

Bossard, James, and Boll, Eleanor S., *One Marriage, Two Faiths* (New York: Ronald Press Co., 1957)

Bowman, Henry A., *Marriage for Moderns* (New York: McGraw-Hill Book Co., Inc., 1960)

Butterfield, Oliver M., *Sexual Harmony in Marriage* (New York: Emerson Books, Inc., 1953)

Child Study Association of America, *What to Tell Your Children About Sex* (New York: Pocket Books, Inc., 1961)

Dickerson, Roy, *So Youth May Know* (New York: Association Press, 1948)

Doniger, Simon L., *Becoming the Complete Adult* (New York: Association Press, 1962)

Dunbar, Flanders, *Your Preteenager's Mind and Body* (New York: Hawthorne Books, Inc., 1962)

Duvall, Evelyn, and Hill, Reuben, *Being Married* (Boston: D.C. Heath and Co., 1960)

Duvall, Evelyn, and Johnson, Joy D., *The Art of Dating* (New York: Association Press, 1958)

Duvall, Evelyn, *Love and the Facts of Life* (New York: Association Press, 1963)

————, *Sense and Nonsense About Sex* (New York: Association Press, 1962)

Eckert, Ralph, *Sex Attitudes in the Home* (New York: Association Press, 1956), out of print

Egleson, Jim and Janet Frank, *Parents Without Partners* (New York: E. P. Dutton & Co., 1961)

Ellis, Albert, *How to Live with a Neurotic* (New York: Crown Publishers, Inc., 1957)

Fedder, Ruth, *A Girl Grows Up* (New York: McGraw-Hill Book Co., Inc., 1957)

Goddard, Carrie Lou, *The Child and His Nurture* (Nashville, Tenn.: Abingdon Press, 1962)

Gottlieb, Bernard S., *What a Boy Should Know About Sex* (Indianapolis, Ind.: Bobbs-Merrill Co., Inc., 1960)

————, *What a Girl Should Know About Sex* (Indianapolis: Bobbs-Merrill Co., Inc., 1961)

Gruenberg, Sidonie, *The Wonderful Story of How You Were Born* (Garden City, N.Y., Doubleday & Co., Inc., Hanover House, 1952)

Hechinger, Grace and Fred, *Teen-Age Tyranny* (New York: William Morrow and Co., Inc., 1962)

Hilliard, Marion, *A Woman Doctor Looks at Love and Life* (Garden City, N.Y.: Doubleday & Co. Inc., 1957)

Jenkins, Gladys G., and Others, *These Are Your Children* (Chicago: Scott, Foresman and Co., 1953)

Johnson, Eric W., *How To Live Through Junior High School* Philadelphia: J. B. Lippincott Co., 1959)

Koonce, Roy F., *Growing with Your Children* (Nashville, Tenn.: Broadman Press, 1963)

Landis, Judson and Mary G., *Teen-Ager's Guide for Living* (Englewood Cliffs, N.J.: Prentice-Hall, Inc., 1957)

Lerrigo, Marion, and Southard, Helen, *Sex Facts and Attitudes* (New York: E. P. Dutton & Co., 1956)

Levy, John, and Munroe, Ruth, *The Happy Family* (New York: Alfred Knopf, Inc., 1962)

Mace, David, *Success in Marriage* (Nashville, Tenn.: Abingdon Press, 1958)

Narramore, Clyde M., *How to Tell Your Children About Sex* (Grand Rapids, Mich.: Zondervan Publishing House, 1958)

Pemberton, Lois, *The Stork Didn't Bring You* (New York: Thomas Nelson & Sons, 1957)

Peterson, James A., *Education for Marriage* (New York: Charles Scribner's Sons, 1956)

Robinson, Marie, *The Power of Sexual Surrender* (Garden City: Doubleday & Co. Inc., 1959)

Shacter, Helen, *Understanding Ourselves* (New York: McKnight, McKnight, 1959)

Stone, Abraham and Hannah M., *A Marriage Manual* (New York: Simon and Schuster, Inc., 1963)

Strain, Frances B., *Being Born* (New York: Appleton-Century-Crofts, Inc., 1954)

Strecker, Edward, and Lathbury, Vincent T., *Their Mother's Daughters* (Philadelphia: J. B. Lippincott Co., 1951)

Suehsdorf, Adie, *Facts of Life for Children*, Child Study Association of America (Indianapolis: Bobbs-Merrill Co. Inc., 1951)

Troelstrup, Arch, *Consumer Problems and Personal Finance* (New York: McGraw-Hill Book Co., 1957)